PATH TO THE LIGHT

Kabbalah Centre Publishing is a registered DBA of Kabbalah Centre International, Inc.

For further information:

The Kabbalah Centre
155 E. 48th St., New York, NY 10017
1062 S. Robertson Blvd., Los Angeles, CA 90035

1.800.Kabbalah www.kabbalah.com

Printed in USA, January 2019

ISBN: 978-1-57189-973-6

eBook ISBN: 978-1-57189-986-6

Design: HL Design (Hyun Min Lee) www.hldesignco.com

PATH TO THE LIGHT

TO THE

DECODING THE BIBLE WITH KABBALAH

KABBALAH CENTRE PUBLISHING

An Anthology
of Commentary
from Kabbalist
Rav Berg

BOOK OF
BERESHEET
Volume 3

Vayetze
Vayishlach
Vayeshev

With much love and appreciation
for my family—past, present and future.
And with gratitude for the merit to help spread
the wisdom of the Rav.

Daniel ben Lazer

PREFACE

In this third volume of commentaries on the Book of Beresheet, Rav Berg deals with the Torah portions of Vayetze, Vayishlach, and Vayeshev. These follow the biblical narrative from Jacob's sojourn with his uncle, Laban, and the journey he takes during which he experiences an extraordinary dream of angels descending and ascending a ladder to Heaven, with God at the top. From here, we follow Jacob back to Canaan with his bride, Rachel; we witness the birth of Joseph, whose father gives him a beautifully colored coat; then there is bitterness caused by hostility between Joseph and his brothers, who eventually sell him into slavery. The story follows Joseph down into Egypt, where he is promoted to master of Potiphar's household, in which Potiphar's wife tries to seduce Joseph; then, when he resists her advances, she has him thrown in jail; and we conclude this volume with Joseph in prison interpreting the dreams of Pharaoh's servants.

These are all intriguing, often salacious and very well-known tales. Yet, as Rav Berg tells us here, they are of no significance and of no spiritual value without the revelation of their coded inner meaning and true message, which only Kabbalah can provide. In Rav Berg's deft hands and nimble mind, Jacob's ladder becomes a cogent explanation for the very structure of reality itself, as well as the means by which the miracle on Mount Sinai came into being, when the blessing of the Torah was given to humankind.

Where the Zohar, quoted extensively here, can often be complicated or oblique with its profoundly metaphysical analyses of the Bible, the Rav is able to succinctly reduce complexity to the most straightforwardly lucid of terms, making it readily intelligible to anyone. For example, he tells us that *sulam*, the Hebrew word for "ladder," has a numerical value of 130, the same value we find in the word *sinai*, making both the metaphor and the practical connection crystal clear. He constantly directs us away from the yarn, which, particularly in these portions, is often puzzling, if not repellent at times, insisting that if the Bible has any value at all it must be of practical use here and now to a world still floundering in chaos and conflict.

If it is to be of true utility, spiritual advice and biblical instruction and information must be easily understood too, and eminently applicable to our daily lives. Kabbalah is solely about the improvement of human life, which will then, in turn, improve the planet. Change begins with us, as the Rav says, "…the world can only be better when there are better people in it."

The most profound wisdom expressed in the simplest terms is the Rav's hallmark, as he explains the teachings of the greatest of sages, the masters of Kabbalah and the holy rabbis, like Rabbi Akiva and Rav Isaac Luria (the Ari), whose words and deeds are often cited here. In the following pages, we find that often baffling and even unsavory stories, familiar to many of us since we were children, blaze into a new life radiant with real meaning, as the Rav demonstrates time and again that the Bible's abstruseness always indicates the presence of a far deeper message and a greater intensity of Light. His discourse on the significance of dots above a word in the Torah Scroll reveals the manner in which a particular energy becomes revealed. He often tells us that without the Zohar, he himself would not have been able to comprehend the true meaning of this ancient text. But in trying to understand the Zohar, without the Rav we would all be rudderless and adrift in an ocean of confusion.

By the end of this volume, we find a whole new world opening up, and the Bible will never be the same again. What was once a stone-like slab or scroll, hauled out and read on Shabbat turns into a transformative blueprint for the salvation of all humanity, as well as of the beautiful blue planet on which we dwell. Finally, we can see why what was formerly just sacred is in fact truly holy, and a timeless, unchanging communication from one generation to the next, heralding the yearned-for Age of the Messiah and a world operating in accordance with Divine laws.

The Rav's analogies, and his simple and often humorous elucidations, make wisdom shine, banishing forever the darkness of ignorance. We are privileged to live at such a time when the gates of Kabbalah are being thrown open by Rav Berg's work.

TABLE OF CONTENTS

BOOK OF BERESHEET:

Portion of Vayetze

PORTION OF VAYETZE

Genesis 28:10 And Jacob left Beersheba and set out for Haran.

Leaving the Past Behind

Immediately preceding this portion of Vayetze was the story of Jacob leaving his father's house in a manner that some say was deceitful. Jacob followed the advice of his mother, Rebecca, to depart from his parents and the land of Israel and journey to his mother's brother, his uncle Laban, to escape from the wrath of his brother Esau. Of course the Bible does not condone such practices, so we know that there is a deeper message here.

In Zohar Chadash, it is explained that the words "coming out of Egypt" are found 50 times in the Bible, and each time we hear those words we are given the opportunity to eliminate our chaos. Regarding the section of Vayetze, the Zohar says that elimination of chaos is the reason a person should leave his father and mother and be with his wife. What does it mean that Jacob left his father and mother? Our parents represent the past. Therefore, it means that we must forget the past and look to the future. As we heard in this first verse, Jacob left Beersheba, which is when he went out of the illusion that was his old life.

11 He reached a certain place, and stayed there for the night because the sun had set, and he took of the stones from there, and put them for his pillows and lay down in that place to sleep. 12 And he dreamed, and saw a ladder set up on Earth, and the top of it reached to Heaven, and he saw the angels of God ascending and descending on it. 13 And behold, the Lord stood above it and said: "I am the Lord, the God of Abraham, your father, and the God of Isaac. The land on which you lie, I will give to you and to your seed; 14 and your seed will be like the dust of the earth, and you will spread to the west and to the east, to the north and to the south; and in your seed will all the families of the earth be blessed. 15 And, behold, I am with you and will watch over you wherever you go, and I will bring you back again to this land, for I will not leave you until I have done what I have promised you." 16 And Jacob awoke from his sleep and said, "Surely the Lord is in this place, and I was not aware of it." 17 And he was afraid and said, "How awesome is this place. This is none other than the House of God; and this is the Gate of Heaven." 18 And Jacob rose up early in the morning and took the stone he had placed as a pillow and set it up as a pillar and poured oil on top of it.

Twelve Special Stones

The Bible tells us, "Jacob took of the stones of that place," yet it does not say how many stones Jacob took. Moreover, why not take just one stone? Surely it would have been more comfortable to lie on one stone than on many pebbles. The Zohar says:

> Notice that it is written, "And he took of the stones of that place," and not, "the stones of the place." THIS MEANS THAT HE CHOSE CERTAIN STONES FROM THERE. HE SAYS, These are precious stones, the twelve supernal pearls, as written, "Twelve stones," (I Melachim 18:31), underneath which are twelve thousands and tens of thousands of polished stones, all of which are called stones. Therefore, the scripture reads, "of the stones," and not, "the stones." The place is the place mentioned, namely, the Nukva.
> —Zohar, Vayetze 1:10

From this Zohar we see that Jacob chose twelve specific stones. In studying Kabbalah, we learn that the number 12 refers to the twelve signs of the zodiac. Here the Bible is not speaking about physical stones but about the constellations. Jacob took these stones, in other words referencing something that will occur in the future.

The literal Biblical story has no meaning for us. We are meant to delve into its deeper implications. We read this story year in and year out, and I must admit that before I entered the world of Kabbalah I ultimately got tired of learning about Jacob bringing forth twelve children with his four wives. Why is the whole story of Jacob and his married life here? What would we miss if we did not know about it? The answer is that the twelve sons relate to the twelve signs of the zodiac. So already there seems to be a connection to what is later described in this portion.

We read the portion year in and year out because Jacob is the seed of the physical manifestation of a connection to the twelve signs of the zodiac. Before the birth of the twelve sons, only Abraham, Isaac, and Jacob could make a connection to the cosmos. No one else could do it. We understand that when we come to the Kabbalah Centre's War Room on Shabbat, we want to connect with the root, the seed of the twelve signs of the zodiac.

In *Sefer Yetzirah*, ("Book of Formation"), Abraham states that the birth of the twelve sons provided humanity, and specifically those who study Kabbalah, with the first opportunity ever available to control each month. The tools we use to capture control at the seed level are the Ana Beko'ach meditation and the connection we make on the first day of each lunar month, known as Rosh Chodesh.

In verse 11, it is written that Jacob had taken "stones," in the plural but in verse 18 of the same chapter, we read that Jacob rose in the morning and took "the stone," in other words, one stone. What happened? Did all of the stones combine into one? Yes.

At birth, each son of Jacob was given the power over one month of the year. The naming of each son was an instrument by which humanity could now tap the positive energy of each month. Through the channels of the twelve sons, we would learn with foresight how to control the influence of each month, so that we do not have to resort to seeing in hindsight all that we could have done differently. When we meditate on the two Hebrew letters that created each month, we connect with the positive energy of that month and thereby ensure control of the Satan. When we make connections, we take control. The twelve sons created control. When they were born, we could thus make this connection to the cosmos through them. There are twelve signs of the zodiac—essentially this means six and six. The first six months are considered the male months, and the second six months are the female months. Meaning that, in the first six months, there is a preponderance of male energy-intelligence; and in the second half of the year—the next six months, there is a preponderance of female energy-intelligence.

The Zohar interprets verse 11 to mean that Jacob took twelve special stones "from that place" (Heb. *makom*). Whenever the word *makom* is used in the Bible, it means Malchut. In other words, it is where things become established, manifested, physically expressed. When we read that Jacob took from the stones of that place, meaning particular stones, it is to indicate to us that that he was preparing for dominion over Malchut, over physicality, over the place where chaos and disorder unfortunately occur.

Jacob lay down on the stones, fell asleep, and dreamt of a ladder. All the commentators explain that this ladder was on the earth and ascended to the Heavens, and that the center of the ladder was directly in line with the place of the Holy Temple. Jacob saw angels ascending and descending on this ladder. Most commentators say that these angels assisted Jacob when he left his father's house, and they accompanied him to the border. When Jacob was outside the territorial boundaries of Israel, the angels took over. This is what some of the commentators who did not study Kabbalah explain. Of course this still does not explain Jacobs's ladder. The ladder has become synonymous with Jacob. What does this mean? Why Jacob? Why a ladder?

Without the Zohar I could not explain why the ladder was so significant. There are so many references to examine here. The Zohar says:

> "And he dreamed, and behold a ladder set up on the earth, and the top of it reached to Heaven." (Beresheet 28:12)
> It is six grades up from the level of a dream, HOD OF

7

THE NUKVA, to the two grades of prophecy, NETZACH AND HOD OF ZEIR ANPIN. The six grades are YESOD OF ZEIR ANPIN, CHESED, GEVURAH, TIFERET, NETZACH, AND HOD OF THE NUKVA. Therefore, a dream is one part out of sixty of prophecy, FOR EACH OF THESE SIX SEFIROT INCLUDES TEN SEFIROT, AND TEN TIMES SIX IS SIXTY. AND A DREAM, WHICH IS THE LOWEST, CONTAINS ONE OUT OF SIXTY. The ladder alludes to him seeing his children receive the Torah on Mount Sinai in the future, because the ladder represents Sinai, for MOUNT SINAI, AS SCRIPTURE READS, "is on the ground," "and its top," NAMELY, ITS HIGHEST POINT, reaches Heaven. And all the Chariots and troops of the High Angels descended there with the Holy One, blessed be He, when he gave them the Torah, as it is written, "the angels of God ascending and descending on it."

—Zohar, Vayetze 11:70

The Zohar is very precise and brief. The Zohar explains that Jacob saw that his children were going to receive the Bible on Mount Sinai. What is the Bible about? Although every verse is totally clouded and abstruse in its meaning, the Bible is still the fundamental body by which we can understand what is happening around us—and it is the basis for the Zohar. The Bible is a cosmic code that teaches us about forces—which forces prevail, when they prevail, which are negative, and which are positive.

The Zohar asks the question: What is the connection between the ladder and the revelation of the Torah, the revelation that would take place in the future on Mount Sinai? The answer is that the ladder is a code for Sinai. Using *gematria* or numerology, we see that the word *sulam* (Heb. for "ladder") adds up to 130, and the word *sinai* adds up to 130. They are equal to each other. What took place on Mount Sinai? Revelation. The Israelites elevated to another level of consciousness, one where death no longer existed. They experienced *bila hamavet laNetzach,* which is immortality. Death refers to a negative energy-intelligence and encompasses all forms of what we consider to be chaos, entropy, decay, and disorder. But with the Revelation on Mount Sinai death came to an end. The Israelites received the instrument, the information by which they could now put an end to chaos and disorder.

The Zohar asks why the Bible tells us that the ladder was *mutzav artza* or "firmly in the earth." Naturally the ladder would be on the ground and not flying in the air. Why did God feel it was so important to tell us that the ladder was on the ground, and that the top reached up to the Heavens? The Zohar explains that "Heavens" is a code for the dimension of Zeir Anpin, and *artza* or *eretz* is a code for Malchut. What Jacob saw in the dream was that it is possible to connect to both realities—Zeir Anpin and Malchut—and that he was being given the instruments and methodology by which he would have total control over this world, the world of the physical Illusionary Reality, as well as the Tree of Life reality that never changes.

Says the Zohar:

> "…and behold the angels of God ascending and descending on it." (Beresheet 28:12) These are the ministers of all the nations who ascend and descend this ladder. When Israel are sinful, the ladder is lowered and the ministers rise. When Israel improve their deeds, the ladder is raised; all the ministers descend and their government is annulled. All depends on this ladder. Here, Jacob saw Esau's government and that of the rest of the nations in his dream.

Another explanation of the verse, "…and behold the angels of God ascending and descending on it," is that the ladder is used to ascend and descend through its top. For when the top, YESOD, is removed, the ladder gives in and all the ministers rule again. When the top is attached again, it is elevated and they all lose their power to govern. All this is one matter, and both explanations are essentially in agreement.
—Zohar, Vayetze 8:53-54

The Zohar states that when the Israelites sin, the ladder goes down and the appointed ones of all the other nations ascend and become rulers. When the Israelites are positive, the ladder rises up and the appointed ones of all the other nations must go down. Because the ladder went up, the appointed ones were no longer connected to the source of energy. What does the Zohar mean by this? Why does it mention that Jacob saw all this while dreaming? Why not simply say that when the Israelites are positive, then they rule, and when the Israelites are negative, the other nations rule. What does it mean that the ladder has to go down or has to go up, and that up and down are dependent upon how the Israelites behave? What does this have to do with the ladder?

This ladder is not just a ladder; rather it behaves like super-strings in physics, elements that connect everyone with everything. The ladder is like the Shield of David, with the Upper and Lower Triad. The Lower Triad is Zeir Anpin, and although Satan has no control in Zeir Anpin, it is where Satan can connect and receive his energy. Satan has no connection to the Upper Triad—which is Abraham (Chesed), Isaac (Gevurah) and Jacob (Tiferet).

When positive actions are performed by the Israelites, the string that connects them to the Upper Triad has dominion and the ladder ascends to the Upper Triad, and then the angels descend. When the

Israelites are negative, the ladder descends and the angels ascend; and this means that the other nations rule because the Israelites are no longer connected and have no security shield. The Zohar explains that when the ladder reaches the Upper Triad, the Israelites can bring down nourishment for themselves and the whole world. When the ladder is lowered, the other nations have dominion because the Israelites are negative and therefore not connected to the Upper Triad.

There is an actual precept for Esau to hate Jacob. Rav Shimon bar Yochai explains that this is because when the Israelite is negative and cannot reach up to receive the nourishment for him or herself, as well as the other nations of the world, the other nations will hate the Israelite.

The Zohar continues:

> "And Jacob awoke out of his sleep, and he said, 'Surely the Lord is in this place; and I knew it not.'" (Beresheet 28:16) HE ASKS, "It is a wonder that he did not conceive such great knowledge?" HE ANSWERS, "The meaning of 'and I (Heb. *anochi*) knew it not' is similar to the meaning of the verse, 'and I have not made supplications to the Lord.'" (I Shmuel 13:12) That is, 'I knew it not' are words of union and devotion, as are the words, 'I have not made supplication.' Jacob said, 'This was all revealed to me, though I have not attentively searched to know THE HOLY NAME *Anochi* (I), WHICH IS THE SHECHINAH, and come under the wings of the Shechinah to become a whole man.'"

> Come and behold. It is written, "...and she said, 'If it be so, why am I (*anochi*) thus.'" (Beresheet 25:22) Rivka [Eng. Rebecca] beheld the Light of the Shechinah daily because the Shechinah was in her tent where she prayed. When

Rivka began to experience the pains of childbirth, it is written, "And she went to inquire of the Lord (*Yud, Hei, Vav,* and *Hei*)." (Beresheet 25:22) She went from the grade of *Anochi* (Lit. I) to the other grade of *Yud, Hei, Vav,* and *Hei.* So *Anochi* is a name of the Shechinah. Therefore, Jacob said, "I have seen so much, yet did not know *Anochi* (I). This is because he was not married and did not yet come under the wings of the Shechinah.

Next, it is written, "And he was afraid, and said, 'How awesome is this place.'" "Place" has two meanings reflecting the two sides. "How awesome is this place," refers to the place he mentioned before, THE SHECHINAH, and to the sign of the Holy Covenant, which must not be annulled.
—Zohar, Vayetze 10:64-66

The Zohar asks why Jacob did not know that this was a holy place. The Zohar answers that the reason Jacob did not know that this place was holy when he awoke was because he did not have that kind of consciousness. We know he did not because he called it "House of God." The Zohar explains that Jacob's consciousness was not elevated because he had not yet married and thus could only reach that level when he got married. The Zohar uses the words *kemo lo cheliti* or "it did not connect." In studying Kabbalah we learn that "knowing" is connection. Jacob had the knowledge, meaning he was aware that this was a holy place but he did not connect to it. It is like people who have information but do not apply it, so it does not become part of them. Connection means that we have the information and we apply it—we make it a part of us. The information might even be in our memory banks but if we do not make a connection to it, if we do not apply it, it is useless to us. Jacob gathered all the information and did not apply it, thus he did not make the connection.

From the above Zohar passages we see that, when Jacob says *anochi lo yadati*, what he means is not that he did not know that this was the place but rather that he did not know that the Shechinah was present there. He did not make the connection with the Shechinah. Rebecca saw the Shechinah all the time because she was an elevated soul and was conscious. When Rebecca felt trouble within her, she sought the *Yud, Hei, Vav* and *Hei*—because *anochi* connects to the lower level, the Shechinah. Jacob did not have to go anywhere to connect with the Shechinah since he had it right there. We all have our own particular Shechinah, our link to existing cosmic intelligences that make us think and act.

For example, someone born in the month of Sagittarius is going to act with all of the negative and positive qualities of Sagittarius. It is beyond their control. When it comes to certain circumstances, we will behave like a programmed robot, nothing less, nothing more. According to the Zohar, we do not make decisions; instead we have been programmed from birth. Based on our prior incarnation, the month we are born in will assist us in fulfillment of our *tikkun*, our spiritual correction—nothing happens by chance. Even what our parents were thinking at the time of intercourse, when we were conceived, is programmed.

Some of us can have doubts even after we come close to the Light and wonder how we can still have negativity around us. Rebecca had no doubts because Rebecca knew that she had to bring these two children into the world. There was a process, and the process must always be beautiful—meaning without judgment in the world. When Jacob said how awesome the place was, it was for only one reason: The Shechinah was there. Through the Shechinah he could have connected to another place, he could have elevated to a higher level; he could have utilized the Shechinah to bring him to another place.

The Zohar continues:

> Although these are two aspects, YESOD AND MALCHUT, they are actually the same. He said, "This is none other than the House of *Elohim* (God)." "This," WHICH IS YESOD CALLED "THIS," must not be neglected; "this" should not be left alone. Its existence is no other than the House of God, WHICH IS THE NUKVA, with which it unites to produce offspring and to pour blessings upon her from all the organs of the body. For this, WHICH IS YESOD, is the Gate to the entire body, WHICH IS TIFERET, as the scripture reads, "and this is the Gate of Heaven." (Beresheet 28:17) THAT IS, TIFERET IS CALLED BOTH "BODY" AND "HEAVEN." Assuredly, this is the Gate to the body by which blessings flow down TO THE NUKVA. It is attached Above TO HEAVEN, WHICH IS TIFERET, and attached Below TO THE NUKVA, WHICH IS CALLED "PLACE," AND ALSO THE "HOUSE OF GOD." HE EXPLAINED, It is attached Above, as it is written, "And this is the Gate of Heaven," AS YESOD IS THE GATE OF TIFERET, WHICH IS CALLED "HEAVEN." It is attached Below, as it is written, "this is none other than the House of God," WHICH MEANS THAT "THIS," YESOD, IS FOUND ONLY IN THE HOUSE OF GOD, WHICH IS THE NUKVA. Therefore, "he was afraid, and said, 'How awesome is this place.'" THE PLACE IS THE NUKVA, AND "THIS" IS YESOD. But men disregard the preciousness OF YESOD, of being perfected through it. The father of the young man went to him and kissed him.
> —Zohar, Vayetze 10:67

The Zohar says that *Elohim* or "God," refers to the lower level of Malchut. The Shechinah, Yesod, and Malchut are all the Gates. The only place we can make connections is through the Gate. If we do not make our connection with the Gate, we will never ascend. Some people strive to reach higher levels, not knowing that we do not work to reach higher levels. There is no such thing as reaching higher levels; we have to work through the Gate and keep making connections to the Gate, opening the Gate. It says in the Zohar that all God asks of us is to "...open to Me an opening no wider than the eye of a needle, and I will open for you the Supernal Gates." This is all that is necessary.

We think we have to be a great *tzadik* (righteous person) to be able to reach such heights and that this requires a lifetime of work—all day and all night, every day. Yet no matter how hard we work, we do not reach such levels. Therefore, the ladder is established and exists right here on Earth. When we climb the ladder, we need to make sure that we can open up the Gates to get all the way up to the Gate of Heaven. And there is only one way to connect to the Gates: We have to restrict and go against the Desire to Receive for the Self Alone. The Zohar explains that it is called the House of God because this is a higher level.

The Malchut level is called the Tree of Knowledge of Good and Evil, not because there is good here but because we can create good here. It is the place where we come to make connections. And to make a connection to the Light requires more than information (Heb. *da'at*). We can be full of information, we may study Kabbalah all our life but if there is no action, no restriction, we have not made a connection. We could learn all about restriction, yet when it comes down to the point where we should restrict, we do not. This is why Jacob said, "I know this is the place of the Shechinah but I did not do anything about it. I did not make the connections to it."

Dreams and Prophecy

The Zohar says that dreams are a form of *nevua* or "prophecy," and they are powerful systems of information—but they have to be read correctly because dreams usually come true. In other words, when we dream, we are getting messages. We are being told of a future because prophecy means that tomorrow is here now. However, there are times when the dream is a fabrication, when it is not true. So how do we know if our dreams are true or not? The Zohar explains that this depends on a person's actions. If their behavior is one of negative activity, if they hate people, if they speak *lashon hara* or "evil speech," if they enact all manner of evil things, then this person will have dreams that will be a total fabrication and have no validity. Such dreams will just awaken fear in the dreamer but have nothing to do with the real future.

Today is the seed of tomorrow and, in studying Kabbalah, we discover that time is an illusion. Einstein agrees with this and further adds that time is mutable and can change. In other words, time is elastic. The reason an evil person will not see tomorrow when they dream is because they are subjected to the world of the Tree of Knowledge of Good and Evil, and thus they cannot connect to the reality called Zeir Anpin—the dimension of the Tree of Life, where there is only good. Unfortunately, those who only live in the physical reality level are subject to good and evil. But there is another reality, called the Tree of Life, and if we live in that reality, then tomorrow is always here today.

When Jacob dreamt, he saw tomorrow as the present. Jacob was being given total dominion over chaos and disorder, which he could see by virtue of this ladder. The Zohar says Jacob saw of Sinai that his children will control the cosmos and that Jacob's dream corresponded to him taking the twelve specific stones, which were not actual stones. The Bible is referring to taking control of the forces of the twelve months that prevail over our lives. It is not saying that Jacob slept on several little stones or even on one stone. This dream, the ladder, and the stones all have significance.

The story of Jacob is talking about gaining control by means of having dominion over the twelve signs of the zodiac. As I mentioned previously, we recite and meditate on the Ana Beko'ach to take control of the positive influences of each month.

Where, when, and how do these twelve stones become one stone? It is very simple—if we have total control over the twelve stones, the twelve signs of the zodiac, then they are as one. It is an illusion that they are twelve separate parts. So there were no longer twelve fragmented frames of time and space in a year. The whole year was the same, was of a constant continuity.

The True Nature of Time, Space and Motion

In Jacob's dream, God told him that the land he lay upon was the land that God would give to him and to his children. All the commentators ask an obvious question: How much land could Jacob have possibly occupied? Even if he were twenty feet tall he could not occupy anything remotely comparable to the size of the entire land of Israel. What kind of assurance was God giving Jacob here? Rashi (Rav Shlomo Yitzchaki, 1040 – 1105), the renowned commentator on the Bible, has an interesting extrapolation on this particular point. He says that the earth curled up under Jacob like a scroll. If we rolled out the Sefer Torah, which is a large scroll, maybe it would stretch for as long as a city block. Now visualize the entire land of Israel curled up into the space Jacob occupied. God promised him the entire land of Israel, not just the area on which he was sleeping. From Rashi, we have here a simple answer to the problem. Yet all the same, do we truly understand what this means?

Rashi, who lived 1,000 years ago, taught that according to the Zohar, time, space, and motion are but an illusion, not a reality. This means that if you are in Los Angeles, at the same time you are also in London and Tokyo. Many would say this is beyond comprehension, yet do we fully understand everything in this universe? No. Many believe that the constructs of the physical world are reality, yet modern physics and the Zohar concur that they are not. We do not understand this because our awareness of reality is veiled and we do not see everything. Often we do not even see what is in front of us. We have all experienced not knowing where our own possessions are in our own homes, have we not?

If we are in Tokyo and want to be in Los Angeles, why do these familiar limitations, such as time and distance, have to be involved? Do we really have to go through the airport security, take our shoes off and go through the whole boarding rigmarole? Kabbalah says we do not have to wait in a long line, we do not have to endure a delay of five hours on the tarmac when, for some reason, the plane cannot take off. The people who perpetuate the illusion that these conditions are the reality are also essentially those who do not behave like Jacob.

Kabbalah teaches that Jacob represents the Central Column. This is a concept that Rav Yehuda Ashlag, founder of the Kabbalah Centre in 1922, presented in his sixteen-volume treatise called the Study of the Ten Luminous Emanations, which describes the Central Column as the principle of Restriction. Exercising the principle of restriction is easier said than done, though. Yet it provides us with everything we hope to achieve in terms of reality. According to Rashi, Jacob removed the curtain of these illusionary concepts, thus preventing them from being a reality. We perpetuate our illusions by our belief in them but the moment we deny their existence, the illusion is gone. Does this mean that now we can be in Los Angeles and in London at the same time, without boarding a plane? The

99 Percent non-physical portion of our being can be there in a split second but because the critical mass necessary to remove the illusion of gravity has not yet been achieved, we still cannot be there completely. Not everyone will be able to accept this principle as easily as Rashi can explain the problem regarding Jacob and his piece of land. To strengthen our convictions, the removal of time, space, and motion is what we are here to achieve—yet it is easier said than done.

In theoretical physics it is claimed that time, space, and motion are an illusion. However, there is a difficulty in proving the theory pragmatically. So it still means that international travel is going to take many hours. Whereas, if the limitations of time, space, and motion did not apply, we could be there in a moment. Why is this? It is because the distance or space that seems to be occupied between each international city is really an illusion. In fact, I can be in London at this moment because London is right here now. I am not saying that everyone must immediately comprehend this idea; I do not believe that even science fully comprehends it. Yet the minute we begin to inject the kind of consciousness that says this cannot be done into the cosmos, we strengthen the concept that time, space, and motion are inevitable limitations, infusing our consciousness with this negative idea.

Jacob understood that the future lay in the removal of these limitations. With this reading is an affirmation that time, space, and motion are simply an illusion. Therefore, when God promised Jacob that the land of Israel would be given to him and his descendants, what God provided was freedom from these hindrances for those who make the effort. This is an effort that requires a great deal of perseverance and a great deal of transformation of our consciousness before it is possible—yet such a revolution in awareness would ultimately benefit all of humanity. The Lightforce of God is ready to help anyone achieve a consciousness that will ultimately eliminate these confines and bring about the true nature of reality. On a very practical level, the elimination of chaos truly can be achieved.

The Bible is teaching us what theoretical physics has of late managed to establish as fact—the distance between two points is an illusion, and every aspect of the physical reality is but interference. This is the real message of this reading. Without energy, the physical reality is an illusion. The only reason travelers still have to take a plane to reach their destination is because we have not yet established mind over matter in our consciousness. Everyone agrees with this but the fact that we can hear these statements is not enough—we need the energy of mind over matter. Where does mind over matter come from? It comes from consciousness—and all we are is only consciousness.

In the same way this seemingly ridiculous chapter tells us that God rolled up the earth, we can understand that the idea of time, space, and motion is a corrupted concept operated by the one who creates all of our chaos—and his name is Satan. He is a force that exists in the universe to inflict pain and suffering on all of humankind.

This story reminds me of how, in the 1990s, war broke out, and Karen and I were invited by the former King of Morocco to visit because he was having his *fête du trône*, which entailed celebrating the day of his father's passing and his accession to the throne. When it was over, we headed to the place where we were staying but the only way to get there was a two lane road out of the city. We had a good number of people from the Centre with us, and we were stuck in a minibus for one hour without moving. Our driver said it would take 24 hours to get to our destination. So I told him we were from the United States and that in New York we have double-decker roadways. I said we were going to meditate for the minibus to take the upper deck of this little highway. To sum it up, I do not know, nor do I care, how it happened but we arrived at the place where we were staying within half an hour!

We have all had miracles happen in our lives but perhaps sometimes we do not pay attention to them. This is why there is a special prayer we recite to appreciate the miracles that occur every day in our lives. When we appreciate miracles, we inject into our consciousness the possibility of miracles happening all of the time.

Jacob's Vision of Angels

There is an unusual infusion of energy that is supplied to us, which we can receive by our participation in this reading. I am also personally pleased with this section since it provides the credibility for our presentation of the Zohar's concepts—concepts that reach deep into the 30th century. This is why The Kabbalah Centre has spearheaded innovation that has trickled down into the scientific world. It is by virtue of our consciousness that the possibility of immortality is now known to humankind. Immortality, which we have chosen as our goal, means the removal of that ultimate threat of death, as well as the chaos-causing doctrine known as time, space, and motion.

Those who study Kabbalah, and who come from a kabbalistic frame of consciousness, accept no part of the Bible on a literal level. We understand that there is a more significant meaning hidden within each letter, each word, each verse. As Rashi said, "God rolled up the entire land of Israel like a scroll and fit it precisely where Jacob lay." What did Rashi mean? Traditionalists believe that one must study Rashi before studying Kabbalah. This is a misrepresentation because Rashi, with his simplicity, is so profound, so deep that it is difficult to understand him without the Zohar. In this emerges another proof of the Centre's view that time, space, and motion are but illusions, an idea which, of course, originated in the Zohar. We are undoing the notion that we must be governed by these limitations. When we inject the consciousness that the limitations of time, space, and motion are an illusion into the cosmos, whether we understand how or why, the illusion will disappear.

In this reading, we have support from the Lightforce of God to help us achieve a consciousness that will erase such limitations, which will enable us to eliminate a fundamental process that sets up chaos.

The Bible says that Jacob dreamt of a ladder along which angels travelled up and down. The Zohar asks why Jacob did not observe the angels coming down and then going up. It appears that the scripture, which states that the angels were "ascending and descending," contradicts what we might speculate about how angels would travel—meaning we believe angels first descend from above and then ascend. Commentators say angels exist above us, and when we call upon our guardian angels, they come down to us from above. What Jacob informed us with his dream is that, in fact, angels are always with us. How do we know this? Rav Isaac Luria (the Ari, 1534 – 1572) says that there are angels for every day of the week. Jacob is teaching us that angels are here and it is possible to connect to them. This is why the codes in the Bible and tools of Kabbalah really exist.

In the dream, God told Jacob that his children shall be as the dust of the earth, they shall spread to all corners of the World, and that he would always be blessed. Jacob awoke from the dream and concluded that this was undoubtedly a place of God, and then he became frightened. How could Jacob have known that this was a place of God? He was sleeping. When we sleep we are unaware of such phenomena. The Bible also adds, "And this is the Gate to Heaven," indicating that the place where Jacob lay must have been a gate, a portal, by which we can reach up into the Heavens.

We all dream every night, yet most of us do not recall our dreams. For Jacob, this dream was extremely important, very real, and the location where he lay when he had the dream was clearly sacred. This was undoubtedly a dream, and yet Jacob understood that it was also a spiritual reality. How many of us would consider such a dream to be reality if we experienced it?

How many of us are confident in the possibility of the elimination of time, space, and motion? How many of us are convinced of our own immortality? We talk about this frequently at The Kabbalah Centre. Science also states that time, space, and motion are illusions. What can be done with this great truth then? This is exactly why the portion of Vayetze exists. At the Kabbalah Centres, we are ridiculed for our statements regarding immortality. I did not realize we would get so much press. If I had the wit of Oscar Wilde I would say, "Just make sure you spell our name correctly."

When the Bible says that Jacob fell asleep, did it mean this literally? What the Bible and the Zohar tell us, and what Rashi implies, is that Jacob did indeed fall asleep but what transpired was not in the realm of sleep. The stories are merely pointing to ideas that can assist us in our daily existence to make life easier. This is the only reason for the Bible's existence. It is not an historical document or a book of laws and rules. Even the Zohar itself states that we could write better stories than those found in the Bible. What the Bible concerns is the realm of consciousness beyond the realm of physicality that, unfortunately for us, coerces our consciousness into beliefs that are illusionary.

When Rashi said that the earth rolled up under Jacob, most of us have trouble believing this, and therein lies our problem. The physical world as we see it is merely a blip on a computer screen. It is there, it comes on, and then it is gone—this is the way science refers to the physical reality. What do we sit on? We sit on atoms—we can sit anywhere, it is the same atom. Ninety-nine percent of Creation is not physical as we understand it; ninety-nine point nine percent of everything in the physical reality is not solid—it is space. In fact, there are more atoms in the air in front of us than there are in a wooden chair, but we cannot feel them.

The story of Vayetze relates the nature of the physical reality, the place where there is no physical liability, restriction or limitation. The limitations of time, space, and motion do not exist. No one in the world would have problems if humankind could overcome the perceived limitations of time, space, and motion. Those able to perceive the problems of tomorrow would know precisely what to do today, and everyone would be content and satisfied on every level. If we could see an impending disaster on an airline, who would go on that plane? How many disasters could we avoid if we were not governed by these limitations? Yet for millennia, we have placed our consciousness completely in the physical reality.

How can a whole land be rolled up? We connect to the Torah on Shabbat to receive the support whereby our consciousness can be elevated. The *only* reality that exists is consciousness—nothing more, nothing less. Whatever is in the mind becomes our reality.

What are we to understand about sleep from Jacob? The Zohar says we are the ones who are asleep, the ones who are not aware. The word "asleep" indicates a lack of awareness. Rav Shimon said that we split the Red Sea every 72 days in our consciousness—so it was easy for the Israelites to perform this miraculous feat. Every permutation of every event happens thousands of times a day. Yet as long as we do not believe we can reverse time and regain our youth, we will never get younger. As long as we fail to believe in ourselves, this faulty belief is endorsed. This is what the whole story of Jacob is about.

Regarding the phrase, "this is the Gate to Heaven," to what is the Bible referring? Where is Heaven? The Zohar says that Heaven is right here, the gate we seek is here. Heaven, like Israel, represents an energy, a consciousness. Heaven is where there are no problems and no limitations, and if those elements are ever experienced, it is not Heaven.

Satan has had a tight hold on humankind for millennia and nothing has changed. If we do not think it can change, it will not change. If we take a look at the past, positive transformation seemed unlikely but in this current age change can happen. People do not ask why the modern age is different. The extraordinary advances of the last century should lead people to ask questions. We flew to the moon, traveled at twice the speed of sound, and how many have asked why this is happening now? No one has asked because we are asleep. This is the power of Satan. We ask why we did not know the reason we did not question—and then along comes the ego to take care of that. We know how to excuse ourselves and our ignorance. But ignorance is no excuse. We need to question everything.

In October 1927, there was a big thrust forward. The Fifth Solvay International Conference on Electrons and Photons was held in Brussels. At this august gathering, the world's most notable physicists and mathematicians met to discuss the newly formulated quantum theory. From this conference emerged a revolution in the understanding of the nature of this world. The leading figures there were Albert Einstein and Niels Bohr. But the only reason I can grasp and embrace such a huge advancement in quantum thought is due to the revealment of the Zohar, which also took place during this period, thanks to the astonishing work of Rav Ashlag. From that moment in the 1920s on, the Zohar was no longer hidden from humanity. Suddenly there was a translation in Modern Hebrew of the original Aramaic text. This is really what made the 20th century so very different from all preceding

centuries. Advancements in understanding are progressing so
rapidly now. Even in the last few years there have been such
dramatic developments in so many fields. Why is this? This is the
common pattern for humanity—then everyone goes back to sleep.
We have the necessary knowledge already; it is not somewhere else,
it is here, and only one thing is missing: humankind's certainty that
immortality is a reality.

God's Promise and Quantum Mechanics

How can it be explained that the entire land of Israel was folded
up? In its explanation for this the Zohar communicates Quantum
Theory. We exist here *and* in Tokyo; everyone is, in fact, able to be
in the same place at the same time. The fact that the whole world
is right here now is, surprisingly enough, not something disputed
by science. Physicists state that the whole universe is connected on
the quantum level; everything is interrelated. They have found out
that atoms can be in ten places at the same time. And because we
are made up of atoms, we, too, can be at many places at the same
time—if we believe enough that it is possible. This idea of quantum
goes back thousands of years; it is a concept from the Zohar that
emerged long before science arrived at its own conclusion in 1927.

If someone tells you they thought they saw you in San Francisco last
week, and then asks if you were there, the answer is that you could
have been there, and indeed elsewhere simultaneously. Science says
that, fundamentally, we can be in all places at all times. Tokyo is
not thousands of miles away; our presence there is only a thought
away. This notion of limitation is merely an illusion. Because our
thinking is mired in time, space, and motion, however, this is
not an easy concept for us to accept. We are fortunate to have a
specific prayer that can take us thousands of miles away. We can
be in Tokyo in our minds using the 99 Percent Reality, which is

consciousness. However, we need 100 percent certainty for this to work 100 percent. At the Kabbalah Centres, we really do believe in the mind over matter principal—the 72 Names of God are our tool for overcoming physicality. This is what we do in Vayetze. We capture and acquire this powerful tool with which we will control time, space, and motion. Surely we have all had enough chaos derived from the physical reality, and we now want to avoid any more coming upon us.

19 And he called that place Bethel, but the name of that city used to be called Luz. 20 And Jacob made a vow, saying, "If God will be with me and will watch over me on this journey I am taking, and will give me bread to eat and clothes to wear, 21 so that I return to my father's house in peace, then the Lord will be my God: 22 and this stone that I have set up as a pillar will be the House of God, and of all that You give me I will surely give one tenth to You."

Establishing Things Below

The sequence of biblical verses above does not appear to be correct. First Jacob makes a vow that if God will be with him, then the Lord will be an *Elohim* (God). He then speaks about the stone pillar that he will set up to indicate that this is a place of God, and concludes by saying that for all God gives him, he will give ten percent (Heb. *aser asrenu*). What does giving ten percent have to do with putting up a stone pillar, and why is it mentioned in between the two other verses? The Bible should just have stated that "God did this for me and I will give ten percent." To answer these questions we will turn to the Zohar, which says:

> "And Jacob vowed a vow, saying, 'If *Elohim* (God) will be with me.'" (Beresheet 28:20) Rav Yehuda said, "Although the Holy One, blessed be He, promised him all that WHEN HE SAID TO HIM, 'AND, BEHOLD, I AM WITH YOU, AND WILL KEEP YOU,' (BERESHEET 28:15) why did Jacob not believe this? Rather, he questioned, 'If *Elohim* will be with me.'?" HE REPLIED, "Only Jacob said, 'I have dreamed a dream, and some dreams are true, and some are

not. If the events in the dream come to pass, then I shall know that the dream is true.' Therefore, he said, 'If *Elohim* will be with me,' as I dreamed, 'then the Lord shall be to me for Elohim; (Ibid. 21); I will draw blessings from the source of the spring of life, BINAH, to the place called Elohim.'"
—Zohar, Vayetze 12:75

Here we see that Jacob is still dreaming, and has not as yet woken up. When he does wake up Jacob says to God, "If you take care of me, I will give ten percent" and yet God did not demand ten percent. It is as though God gives Jacob a free trip, with no conditions. So often it seems to us that God does not help because we do not get what we want. However, we do get what we need. When we do not receive help from another source—the doctor, economist, social worker, psychiatrist, rabbi, priest—we seek God. But God already told Jacob in the dream, "I will do everything for you, without demanding anything in return." So why does Jacob then demand of God, "Fulfill my demands, God, and then I will take care of you."?

The Zohar asks why Jacob did not believe that God would fulfill all His promises. And then the Zohar answers that sometimes dreams are true and sometimes they are false. Dreams that are true are part of prophecy and can teach us about the future, as well as about a prior incarnation. This is because prophecy rises above time, space, and motion. But there are times when our dreams do not reveal the future. The Zohar explains that our dreams are dependent on our actions: If during the day we are engaged in negative behavior, we are given dreams that are false. Jacob knew that some dreams are true, and then there are some dreams that are not true. Jacob was not doubting God, he was doubting whether the dream he had dreamt was indeed true. The Zohar explains:

Come and behold, Israel, NAMELY, THE CENTRAL COLUMN, who is in the middle of everything, receives plenty first from the source of life, BINAH. What he receives, he draws to the place, THE *NUKVA*. This is understood from the verse that begins, "then the Lord shall be to me," WHICH MEANS THAT HE IS THE FIRST TO RECEIVE and continues, "for *Elohim*," WHICH IS THE NUKVA. THIS MEANS THAT HE WILL THEN PASS IT TO THE NUKVA. As *Elohim* will preserve me and do all this kindness by me, so will I draw from my place, NAMELY, ZEIR ANPIN, all these blessings, and the general connection, YESOD, will be tied to it. When will that be? In time, "so that I come back to my father's house in peace," (Beresheet 28:21) which means when I will be perfect in my grade, TIFERET, and perfect in the grade of peace, YESOD, to correct "my father's house," WHICH IS THE NUKVA, CALLED "HOUSE." "I come back in peace" is precise, ALLUDING TO YESOD; "then the Lord shall be to me for *Elohim*."
—Zohar Vayetze 12:76

The Zohar continues with the explanation that when Jacob accepted the responsibility to activate the Central Column (restriction) with his behavior, he received nourishment from the wellspring of Binah, the storehouse of all the blessings. He then drew all of these blessings down and brought them to the world of action, our world. When the Zohar says, "then the Lord (*Yud, Hei, Vav* and *Hei*) shall be to me for *Elohim* (God)," this means that Jacob would bring the *Yud, Hei, Vav,* and *Hei* down to the level of Malchut. Jacob was saying that all of these things in the dream that God said He will provide are dependent on one thing—that Jacob will establish the stone pillar (Heb. *matzeiva*) on the level of *Elohim*. What does "establish the stone" mean? *Matzeiva* comes from the words *mutzav artza*, meaning "the place where things are established."

The Zohar explains that while we have to connect with the realm of Binah to make a connection, things are not established in the Upper Level of Binah, but rather things are established in the Malchut level, our physical world. We can only connect with the Light if we have established things in the right way here on this physical level or, in other words, that we have acted with restriction. This is what Jacob meant. He understood that when he makes all the right connections on the physical level, then he knows that he is bringing Binah, or the *Yud*, *Hei*, *Vav*, and *Hei*, down to this level and "then the Lord shall be to me for *Elohim*." The Bible is not only discussing Jacob here. This is a code for human behavior. The Bible is teaching us about the true nature of our actions. These are the secrets of how to achieve connection and create the miracles that Jacob is destined to receive.

There are so many lessons for us to learn from this section. When Jacob states, "It is going to be for me," this is to indicate that we cannot share that which we do not have. Jacob could not draw the energy down if he was not complete. First, we draw this energy to ourselves, and we can only do this by working on ourselves. If we are unable to perform the elementary restrictions necessary, then we will not make any connection to Binah. Unless we are working to reach the level where action is supposed to take place, all the blessings we are looking for can never come down.

What does Jacob mean by saying, "so that I can come back to my father's house in peace."? The Zohar explains this to mean that when Jacob comes to peace with himself, then he can return to his father's house. It is not about God giving him peace. God can give us peace every single day. He furnishes everyone with all they need. But there is one problem—it is here but we are not connected to it. When Jacob was whole with himself and could sit in peace, only then could he return home. When we are whole within ourselves, then our household, everything around us, will be at peace. If we are not at peace with ourselves, then we will never create an atmosphere of peace. This is such a fundamental and vital teaching.

A person who does not have any doubts, when he goes through pain, is truly at peace with himself. He understands that this is a process, and he knows why he is part of the process. In the case of Rabbi Akiva (Akiva ben Yosef, 50 AD – 137 AD), even as the Romans removed the flesh from his body, he was so happy because he knew that he was paying the debt from his previous incarnation as Issachar, one of the brothers who sold Joseph into slavery. He was at peace with himself because now the cosmos would be free of another liability against humankind. The sale of a brother into slavery is a serious error, and Rabbi Akiva took upon himself the entire encapsulation of this kind of negativity, and he removed it. Rabbi Akiva felt the pain only for one second, and then there was no more pain, just peace because he was happy for this opportunity to remove and eradicate forever his part of the negativity that was brought on by the sale of Joseph. The Romans believed they were causing Rabbi Akiva pain by torturing him to death but it was an illusion.

When we are not at peace with ourselves it is because we have doubts. We blame God. We do not look inside to understand, to see that maybe there is a reason, a purpose for experiencing this pain. By saying that God is with him in Malchut, when he sits in peace, Jacob is reminding us that God is always here with us when we are at peace with ourselves.

The Zohar tells us:

> Another explanation for: "So that I come back to my father's house in peace." There, "IN MY FATHER'S HOUSE," is the Holy Land, where I will be perfected and "the Lord

shall be to me for *Elohim*." In that place I will properly rise from this grade to another, where I will worship Him.
—Zohar, Vayetze 12:77

Does the above passage mean that when we get to Israel, we will have peace? No, not necessarily. So what does it mean? Regarding the meaning of connecting. Jacob was connected to Israel even while he was outside of Israel because he was already in his father's house.

Now we can understand why Jacob speaks about establishing a stone pillar right in the middle of this dialogue with God. When someone departs from this world, we erect a stone at the gravesite, and we perform the unveiling of the stone. We reveal it, not because we are removing the covering off of the stone but because we are establishing its connection. When we want to connect with the energy of a *tzadik* (righteous person) who has left this world, we visit their gravesite. The stone is the wellspring of the Light of the *tzadik*; it is the Foundation Stone (Heb. *Even Shtiya*).

Jacob made peace with himself to teach us that when we are at peace with ourselves, we connect with this world, connect with the energy of restriction, which is essentially all that it is about, and then we have made a House of God and then the *Yud, Hei, Vav,* and *Hei* will become a God for us.

The Zohar says:

> Similarly, Jacob TOO WAS AFRAID THAT HE MIGHT SIN, AND THAT BECAUSE OF THE MANY WICKED IN THE WORLD, THE FLAW WOULD REACH THE NUKVA. Therefore, he did not trust THE PROMISE OF THE LORD THAT WAS GIVEN HIM. However, do not say that he did not trust the Holy One, blessed be He. It is not

so. He simply did not believe in himself, and he was afraid that he might sin AND THAT HIS SIN, TOGETHER WITH THE OTHER SINS IN THE WORLD, would prevent him from returning home in peace. And as a result, the keeping would be removed from him. Therefore, he did not trust himself. "And the Lord will be to me for *Elohim*" means when I will return in peace, I will put even mercy before judgment, so I will worship Him always.
—Zohar, Vayetze 12:75

From the Zohar, we see that Jacob did not doubt God; he doubted himself, doubted his own behavior. If our behavior during the day was one of negative activity, where our vibrations, impressions, and relationships, specifically with people, were of a negative nature, and then we dream that night, the dream is not true. However, if that day we were successful in our correction (Heb. *tikkun*) and behaved in a positive manner, we should know that if we dream that night, the dream will be true and we will have been blessed with a form of prophecy.

Jacob said, "And everything you give me, I will give ten percent." With this the Bible is telling us that there is a process by which we facilitate the coming into our world of the *Yud*, *Hei*, *Vav*, and *Hei*. When we are at peace, with restriction, the minimum that is required is to establish the aspects of the Right Column and the Central Column. We establish the Right Column by sharing. The first of anything we get goes to God. What does this mean? Does God need it? No, it is to indicate our effects on the Malchut level—which is active sharing.

With regard to the ten percent, the Bible is not specific. All it says is "I will make the *aser* (a tenth) for You." It does not say, "I will give." But since this really does not make sense, the commentators say it means ten percent. The Zohar explains that the word *eser* (ten) is a code for Malchut and that Jacob is referring to the World of Asiya—our level of existence. In this world, there is only one aspect we have at our disposal, and that is our ability to restrict negative activity, which is the essence of free-will. Nothing more, nothing less. Everything else is programmed, predetermined, except for the transformation of the Desire to Receive for the Self Alone into the Desire to Receive for the Sake of Sharing. That is all; it is everything we need to do. Therefore, the Zohar says, *aser aseren* has nothing to do with giving ten percent to charity. It has to do with human behavior, with human control. Instead of living in misery and chaos, restriction gains for us the ability to move to another level of consciousness, closer to the Tree of Life Reality—and we can alter our program by restricting.

In this section, Jacob was discovering his first lesson. When God told Jacob, through prophecy, that He was going to give him all these good things, Jacob wondered how to ensure that tomorrow is going to have no ups and downs. The ultimate conclusion of any venture, of any endeavor, is restriction. This is why Jacob said he was going to take *aser* (a tenth) and turn it around. He would give it himself. There is the *Or Yashar* (Direct Light) and *Or Chozer* (Returning Light). Jacob would take the tenth Sefira, Malchut, and turn it from being the tenth Sefira into the seed of all Ten Sefirot—an entirely different denomination. This is how he knew for sure that God would be with him.

Where was God during the Holocaust? Where is God in our daily lives when we experience chaos and disorder? The answer is that God is here all the time, waiting for us to call on Him. God is giving us the free-will we demanded at the time of the Original Restriction—the *Tzimtzum*. We demanded the ability to participate in the entire scheme of things. We did not want to be robots, as we were in the Endlessness. We wanted the opportunity to participate, to be in a position where we could make things happen. In this way

God could be with us all the time. We achieve this by the restriction of Malchut, transforming the Desire to Receive for the Self Alone into one of Desire to Receive for the Sake of Sharing.

After Jacob made this connection, he was sure that God would help him. Making a connection means actively participating, like the filament in the light bulb that pushes back the electric current, causing the light to exist. Jacob was not talking about charity; he was talking about transforming the Desire to Receive for the Self Alone into one of Sharing.

Jacob Swore to Give

Would Jacob only give a tithing with certain conditions attached to it? This is a common way of looking at the account. Do many of us not say that we will give money when God improves our health, our finances, and so on? Yes. The Zohar says that this is not what Jacob meant, though. Jacob's story teaches us about the laws of tithing. We understand tithing to be a mandatory giving of ten percent of what we earn, without any conditions. Yet it seems from this section that tithing actually can be conditional.

Jacob said that if God gave him food and clothing, and returned him back to the house of his father, and if God was always with him through all of this, he would offer a tithe. It seems as if Jacob made a pact with God to first see the results, and only then would he act correctly.

Our actions are ruled by the laws of physics. To cross a twenty-yard street, we must first take a step. We would never reach to the other side if we stopped to calculate how much distance is involved. These are the restrictions of time, space, and motion.

It is normal for someone to be unsure but we are discussing the Patriarch Jacob here—so this does not make sense. Jacob was someone with a constant connection to the Flawless Universe, a dimension where there is no chaos, while he was still living in this world. Can any of us change our destiny under the influence of energy channeled through the stars, and make a pact with God the way Jacob did? What the Bible is teaching us about Jacob is not that he doubted tithing but that he knew there is a Flawless Universe.

What is the reason for giving ten percent? Rav Shimon explains that we have to get out of the clutches of this physical universe, and that tithing is a way of breaking free of our physical limitations and our own baser nature. Jacob knew that he had to remove himself from the material sphere, and that the ten percent really belongs to Satan. I certainly do not want it. We can say that everything we want and need is ours but we still have to disconnect from the physical reality. The Flawless Universe is the true reality—this is what Jacob is telling us.

Beresheet 29:1 Then Jacob went on his journey and came to the land of the people of the east. 2 And he looked and saw a well in the field, and there were three flocks of sheep lying near it, for out of the well they watered the flocks. And a great stone was over the mouth of the well. 3 And all the flocks were gathered there, and they rolled the stone from the well's mouth and watered the sheep, and put the stone again over the well's mouth in his place. 4 And Jacob said to them, "My brothers, where are you from?" And they said, "We're from Haran." 5 And he said to them, "Do you know Laban, the son of Nahor?" and they said, "We know him." 6 And he said to them, "Is he well?" And they said, "He is well. See, here comes Rachel, his daughter with the sheep." 7 And he said, "Look the day is still high; it is not time for the cattle to be gathered together; water the sheep and go and feed them." 8 And they said, "We cannot, until all the flocks are gathered and till they roll the stone from the well's mouth, then we water the sheep." 9 And while he was talking with them, Rachel came with her father's sheep, for she kept them. 10 And it came to pass, when Jacob saw Rachel, daughter of Laban, his mother's brother, and the sheep of Laban, his mother's brother, he went near and rolled the stone from the mouth of the well and watered the flock of Laban, his mother's brother. 11 And Jacob kissed Rachel and raised his voice and wept. 12 And Jacob told Rachel that he was her father's brother

**and that he was Rebecca's son; and she ran
and told her father. 13 And it came to pass,
when Laban heard the news of Jacob, his sister's son, he ran to meet him, and embraced
him and kissed him and brought him to his
house, and he told Laban all these things.**

Secret of the Well

The Zohar says:

The verse, "And he looked, and behold a well in the field,"
contains a secret. For he saw that the Upper Well, THE
NUKVA, resembled THE LOWER OTHER WELL,
WHICH WAS IN TUNE TO IT. As it is written, "and
lo, there were three flocks of sheep lying by it." (Beresheet
29:2) THIS MEANS THAT THE THREE FLOCKS
OF SHEEP ARE CONSTANTLY AT THE MOUTH
OF THE WELL. HE ASKS, "If there are three, why is it
later written, 'And there all the flocks gathered,' WHICH
MEANS THAT THERE ARE MORE HERDS?'" HE
ANSWERS, "There are three AND NO MORE, south,
east, and north NAMELY, CHESED, GEVURAH AND
TIFERET. South is on the RIGHT side, north on the LEFT
side, and east is THE CENTRAL COLUMN between
them. And those who stand on this well and join it, fill it.
Why DO THEY WATER IT? Because, 'for out of that well
they watered the flocks,' THAT IS, THE LOWER SOULS
OF BRIYAH, YETZIRAH, ASIYAH, as it is written,
'they give drink to every wild beast,' (Tehilim 104:11)
WHICH ARE THE SOULS OF BRIYAH, YETZIRAH
AND ASIYAH. IN THAT WAY, HE EXPLAINS THE
VERSE, "AND THERE WERE ALL THE FLOCKS

GATHERED," WHICH MEANS ALL THE SOULS OF BRIYAH, YETZIRAH AND ASIYAH. BUT ONLY THREE WATER THE WELL THE THREE COLUMNS CHESED, GEVURAH AND TIFERET."
—Zohar, Vayetze 14:92

The Zohar tells us what took place at the well is a secret. When Jacob saw the well he immediately recognized that the well was the Gate to the Upper Worlds. It is written that there were three flocks. This indicates that if we want to connect to and draw from the well of blessings, the well has to be established with the Three Columns: Chesed, Gevurah, and Tiferet. Then we can furnish blessings for ourselves, and for others. Without a need of some kind, there is no activity.

The Bible is not telling us that Jacob had enormous strength and could do what all the others in the world could not do, but rather that without Jacob, without the Central Column—the balance of Three Columns—they could not uncover the well. What that means for us on a practical level is that in this physical world, when we have established the Three Columns within ourselves, then we open up the well of blessings, not only for ourselves but for everyone.

The Zohar continues:

> Come and behold, when Jacob, who sat upon the well, saw the water rising up to him, he knew he would meet his wife there. After Moses, who also sat upon the well, saw the water rising toward him, he too knew his wife would come there. And so it was that Jacob met his wife there, as it is written, "And while he was still speaking with them, Rachel came with her father's sheep.... And it came to pass, when Jacob saw Rachel." It is also written of Moses, "And the

shepherds came and drove them away...." (Shemot 22:17)
And there he met Tziporah, his wife. This well caused all
of this BECAUSE THE WELL IS THE SECRET OF
THE SUPERNAL NUKVA. THUS, THEY MET THE
NUKVA OF THIS WORLD.
—Zohar, Vayetze 14:95

Jacob connected to the well and because of this connection, all that
he was looking for came forward to him. This is what is required
of us. To be with the Light takes more than simply saying we are
with the Light. Everything in this world is here by virtue of effort.
Everything in this world involves action. When we have prepared
ourselves spiritually, and when we are at peace within, then
everything will come to us. We prepare Malchut, and when the
Malchut is ready, then the blessing comes; the water rises on its own,
as the water from the well did. There is no necessity to pump it or
draw it up mechanically.

Come and behold, this word "well" is mentioned in this
text seven times because seven IS THE NUKVA OF
ZEIR ANPIN, THE SECRET OF SEVEN, WHICH
INCLUDES SEVEN SEFIROT. It also alludes to Beer
Sheva (lit. "a well of seven"). HE EXPLAINED THAT this
"well" is mentioned seven times in this text, as it is written,
"And he looked, and behold a well in the field... for out of
that well... and a great stone was upon the well's mouth
and they rolled the stone from the well's mouth and put
the stone back upon the well's mouth and still they roll the
stone from the well's mouth and rolled the stone from the
well's mouth." There are seven mentions. Assuredly this is
so because it includes seven grades.

In the text about Moses, THE WELL is mentioned only
once, as it is written, "and dwelt in the land of Midian, and

he sat down upon a well." (Shemot 2:15) This is because
Moses renounced his house Below. Jacob, HOWEVER, did
not renounce his house Below at all. Therefore, a well is
mentioned only once in regard to Moses, as it is written,
"My dove, my undefiled is but one; she is the only one of her
mother." (Shir haShirim 6:9) Therefore, Moses is the owner
of the house, as his root is Above the lower Nukva called
"house" and he rose above it. Therefore, it is written of
Moses, "and he sat down upon a well," THAT IS, ABOVE
THE WELL. Of Jacob it is written, "And he looked, and
behold a well in the field," and not "and he sat down upon
a well."
—Zohar, Vayetze 14:96-97

The significance of the number seven is completeness, like Jacob.
Jacob remained with Rachel (who represented Malchut) until her
passing, and then he ascended to another level. Moses was different
because he had left Tzipora and the world of Malchut, and was
not involved with the seven Sefirot of Beer Sheva (*sheva* in Hebrew
means "seven"). Therefore, the word "well" is mentioned only with
regard to Moses to indicate to us that he knew he would ultimately
leave the world of Beer Sheva, the completeness of Malchut.

The Meaning of Wells

The well plays such a significant role in the Bible. Everyone meets
at a well: Abraham had disputes over the well; Moses, Isaac, and
Jacob meet their future wives at a well. Is it so important that we
know where they met their wives? As the Zohar reveals, the well
is referring to the access of the aspect of anti-matter. I would urge
those unfamiliar with this subject to pursue research into anti-
matter because it is the key to our survival. The Kabbalah Centre is
working on so many fronts to improve the quality of life around the

entire world. We are not only employing people within the Centres, we are also working together with scientists, heads of government, and heads of large corporations to bring an understanding of the importance of releasing a greater quantity of anti-matter into this universe. While we are successful in these endeavors, it is certainly not enough. We still live in a completely polluted environment. I read reports from all over the world, and I have begun to understand that today we do indeed exist in a world that is increasingly unfit for human habitation. We have the opportunity to reveal more about anti-matter by virtue of this aspect known as "the well."

Water is the only compound on a physical level that defies the laws of nature. Water contradicts the accepted natural laws and principles of this world. This story teaches us that the physical laws of nature only exist as long as we believe in them. Water defies the laws of nature that are normally bound up with the limitations of time, space, and motion. The laws of nature are not real; they are a concoction of Satan. For those of us who study Kabbalah, we attest that there is no other way to see the world. When we connect to the reading of Jacob meeting Rachel at the well, we are imbued with the essence of water, which defies the laws of nature, and we are thus provided with the strength to defy the laws of nature.

Unlike the physical process required to draw water from a well—a bucket on a long rope and the effort of drawing water up in it—the Zohar explains that for Jacob, the waters rose up on their own. The same thing happened for Eliezer when he sought a wife for Isaac. He knew that he would meet Isaac's wife at the well, just as Jacob met Rachel, because the waters rose by themselves. Here, the Bible is teaching us the power of water. There is ordinary water and there is anti-matter water, which goes against the limitations of this world, defying the basic characteristic of this universe, which is that of gravity. Gravity is what prevents a person from being in London or Tokyo in a minute. The power of water is that it is able to rise against the natural laws of this universe (gravity) since we see it on a physical level. Gravity is indeed an illusion.

Interestingly enough, the Zohar states that when Jacob approached Rachel, a stone covered the well. One of the shepherds explained that they could not remove the stone from the mouth of the well until all the shepherds gathered together to roll it away. The Bible states that, as Jacob was speaking, he saw Rachel and *vayagel*, he "rolled" over the stone that was covering the well. The Zohar asks a very simple question: why does the Bible use the word *vayagel* instead of the word *vayikach*, meaning he "removed" the stone? The Zohar makes a distinction between the two words and explains that, if the only intention was to remove the stone, then there would be an action—removing the stone and putting it in another location. To "roll" over indicates that there is continual movement from one place to another. The Zohar gives us an incredible interpretation: Jacob knew the water was elevating and thus he created this consciousness because he wanted to have Malchut under control. The water was under Jacob's control. Although it rose up by itself, it was a result of his presence. It seems that this was not sufficient for Jacob, who personally rolled over the stone. He was not going to let God do the work for him.

14 And Laban said to him, "Surely you are my bone and my flesh." And Jacob stayed with him for a whole month. 15 And Laban said to Jacob, "Because you are my brother, should you work for me for nothing? Tell me what your wages should be." 16 And Laban had two daughters; the name of the older was Leah, and the name of the younger was Rachel. 17 Leah was tender-eyed, but Rachel was beautiful and well favored. 18 And Jacob loved Rachel and said, "I'll work for you seven years in return for Rachel, your younger daughter." 19 And Laban said, "It is better that I give her to you than to some other man. Stay here with me." 20 And Jacob served seven years for Rachel, and they seemed like only a few days to him because of his love for her. 21 And Jacob said to Laban, "Give me my wife, for my days are fulfilled so that I may go in unto her."

Seven Years

The Zohar says:

> Come and behold. It is written, "I will serve you seven years for Rachel your younger daughter." (Beresheet 29:18) HE ASKS, "Why did Jacob say 'seven years' instead of ten months or one year?" HE ANSWERS, "Jacob acted wisely so that people would not say that he lusted after Rachel's beauty but WOULD KNOW that he acted wisely. For the moon, THE NUKVA OF ZEIR ANPIN, is seven years old, MEANING IT NEEDS TO BE BUILT BY THE

SEVEN SEFIROT: CHESED, GEVURAH, TIFERET, NETZACH, HOD, YESOD, AND MALCHUT. And all the seven upper years CHESED, GEVURAH, TIFERET, NETZACH, HOD, YESOD AND MALCHUT OF BINAH rested on Jacob before he married Rachel so that they would suit her properly, THAT IS, GIVE OF THE SEVEN SEFIROT OF BINAH TO HER SEVEN SEFIROT. For at first Jacob took everything FROM BINAH and then he came to her, so that he should be CONSIDERED AS ZEIR ANPIN, the Heaven, and she should be CONSIDERED THE NUKVA OF ZEIR ANPIN, the Earth."
—Zohar, Vayetze 16:128

The Zohar says the reason Jacob said he would work for Laban for seven years is to indicate that he was doing so not only because Rachel was beautiful but that there was a higher purpose, too. The Bible wants to teach us that in everything there will be a process, no matter what we do. Naturally, many of us would like the process to reach its objective yesterday. But nothing happens this way in this world; everything must go through a process. Someone could be working for years and be with the Light, and still nothing is happening. The lesson the Zohar wants to teach us is that unfortunately most of us think that the goal is the goal. We do not understand that the process is the goal. Meaning, what is at hand is the goal because a process could take more than a lifetime to complete.

We are mistaken when we think we have accomplished our goals in life. We never get to our goal because the process is the goal. The Zohar wants to teach us that the end of the road is the first step; this step is the end of the road, and every other step we take is part of the end of the road.

22 And Laban gathered together all the men of the place and made a feast. 23 And it came to pass in the evening that he took Leah, his daughter, and brought her to Jacob, and he went in unto her. 24 And Laban gave to his daughter Leah, Zilpah his servant girl, as her handmaid. 25 And it came to pass that in the morning, behold it was Leah; and he said to Laban, "What is this you have done to me? Did I not serve you for Rachel? Why have you deceived me?" 26 And Laban said, "It is not a custom in our country to give the younger before the firstborn. 27 Fulfill her week; and we will give you this also for the service of another seven years of work." 28 And Jacob did so. He fulfilled her week, and he gave him Rachel, his daughter, to wife also. 29 And Laban gave to Rachel, his daughter, Bilhah, his handmaid, to be her maid. 30 And he went in also unto Rachel, and he loved Rachel more than Leah, and served with him yet another seven years. 31 And when the Lord saw that Leah was hated, he opened her womb, but Rachel was barren. 32 And Leah conceived and gave birth to a son. And she named him Reuben, for she said, "Surely the Lord has seen my affliction. Now therefore my husband will love me." 33 And she conceived again, and gave birth to a son and said, "Because the Lord heard that I am hated, he has also given me this son." And she named him Shimon. 34 And she conceived again, and gave birth to a son and said, "Now this time my husband will be joined to me, because I have borne

him three sons." So she was named Levi. 35 And she conceived again, and gave birth to a son and she said, "Now I will praise the Lord." So she named him Yehuda and left bearing.

Beresheet 30:1 And when Rachel saw that she was not bearing Jacob any children, Rachel envied her sister, and said to Jacob, "Give me children, or else I die." 2 And Jacob's anger was kindled against Rachel and he said, "Am I in the place of God, who has kept you from the fruit of your womb?" 3 And she said, "See my maid Bilhah, go unto her and she shall bear upon my knees that I may also have children by her. 4 And she gave him Bilhah her handmaid as a wife, and Jacob went in unto her. 5 And Bilhah became pregnant and bore Jacob a son. 6 And Rachel said, "God has judged me; and he has also heard my voice and has given me a son." Therefore, she named him Dan. 7 And Bilhah, Rachel's maid conceived again and bore Jacob a second son. 8 And Rachel said, "I have wrestled a great struggle with my sister, and I have won." And she named him Naphtali. 9 When Leah saw that she had stopped having children, she took Zilpah, her maid, and gave her to Jacob as a wife. 10 And Zilpah, Leah's maid, bore Jacob a son. 11 And Leah said, "A troop comes." So she named him Gad. 12 And Zilpah, Leah's maid, bore Jacob a second son. 13 And Leah said, "Happy am I, for

the daughters will call me blessed." And she named him Asher.

The Children of Jacob, the Zodiac, and the Birth of the Twelve Tribes

At this point in the story, the children of Jacob are born, and it is clear what they represent. Jacob had four wives, who between them had twelve children, and each child represents a sign of the zodiac. We are influenced by the stars—we can be subject to the negative aspect or else be connected to the positive.

All the biblical stories point to humankind's potential to have dominion over the laws of nature—like time, space, and motion—and the influence of the planets. When we study Kabbalah, we discover there are universal spiritual laws that we must adhere to, laws that are independent of the physical ones. What are the universal laws we must adhere to? "Thou shall not steal," for example. However, this law refers to more than property. And "Thou shalt not kill" refers to more than the elimination of life from the body of another. A person can steal an idea, and you can murder a person with words in the form of gossip. These are the spiritual laws that cannot be broken without consequence.

The section that describes the birth of Jacob's children refers to aspects of nature—the signs of the zodiac and the influence of the stars—that we can change. We can alter the influence of the physical universe. This power was given to man; it was given to Adam at the time of his birth. These miraculous powers are meant to be the norm and are not a cause of the pain and suffering we all experience. Pain and suffering are an illusion; they do not exist. Does disease, therefore, not exist? It exists only to the extent that an individual believes it exists. Scientists have taken a long time to arrive at this conclusion, but they are gradually coming to accept it.

14 During the days of the wheat harvest, Reuben went out into the fields and found mandrakes, and he brought them to his mother Leah. Then Rachel said to Leah, "Give me, I pray you, of your son's mandrakes." 15 And she said to her, "Is it a small matter that you have taken my husband? Will you take my son's mandrakes too?" And Rachel said, "Very well, he can lie with you tonight in return for your son's mandrakes." 16 And Jacob came in from the fields that evening, and Leah went out to meet him and said, "You must come in unto me for I have hired you with my son's mandrakes." And he lay with her that night.

The Wives Trade Jacob for Flowers

Rachel, who had no children, asked Leah to give her the mandrakes, and in exchange she would let Leah sleep with Jacob that night. It is extraordinary, the things that happen in the Holy Bible! How many of us knew about this story before now? Only when we study Kabbalah do we learn that anyone reading the Bible literally is considered foolish. This is what the Zohar said more than two thousand years ago. However, because Kabbalah has been withheld, the world did not have the code by which to comprehend the concealed Bible teachings. Everything in this portion and the next—Vayishlach—cannot be understood without a decoding instrument. Nothing in this portion should be considered as literal reality. What the Zohar reveals are the secrets of the universe whereby the Tree of Life consciousness can be achieved, and will pervade our entire being. This wisdom of Kabbalah was never intended to be a religion but rather something through which we can attain harmony with the universe.

We need to know how many children Jacob had because God created within each month an opportunity to tap into a specific energy that flows at that time. In this portion, we have an opportunity to access the energy of free-will that God infused this universe with at the time of Creation—an energy that would permit mankind to overcome chaos.

The mandrake flower and the story of the twelve sons teach us that we have to infuse our actions with positive energy. This is why Vayetze exists, to give us all a little infusion of energy.

17 And God listened to Leah, and she became pregnant and bore Jacob a fifth son. 18 And Leah said, "God has rewarded me for giving my maidservant to my husband." And she named him Issachar. 19 And Leah conceived again and bore Jacob a sixth son. 20 And Leah said, "God has presented me with a precious gift. Now my husband will dwell with me, because I have borne him six sons." And she named him Zebulun. 21 And afterward she gave birth to a daughter and named her Dinah.

The Birth of Dinah

In this section, Leah became pregnant and prayed. Through her prayers, she changed the sex of the fetus within her womb from male to female, thus giving birth to a baby girl, whom she named Dinah. The commentators tell us that the important point here is that the sex of the fetus was changed within her womb. Such an act cannot be performed unless all the accumulated detritus of the former identity is washed away. This would require a return to the very beginning of a soul's existence, before there was even a physical world. This is the only way that such a state of freedom can be achieved. It is so difficult for us to change, but we can go back in time and lose all the accumulated baggage. We will wash away something simply by connecting with this reading. How much we have washed away depends entirely on each individual's efforts. The advantage is that what we have gained will be there.

22 And God remembered Rachel; and God hearkened to her and opened her womb. 23 And she conceived and gave birth to a son and said, "God has taken away my reproach." 24 She named him Joseph, and said, "The Lord shall add to me another son." 25 And it came to pass when Rachel gave birth to Joseph that Jacob said to Laban, "Send me on my way so I can go back to my own place and to my own country. 26 Give me my wives and children, for whom I have served you, and let me go, for you know how much work I've done for you." 27 And Laban said to him, "I pray you, if I have found favor in your eyes, please stay. I have learned by experience that the Lord has blessed me because of you." 28 And he said, "Name your wages, and I will give it." 29 And he said to him, "You know how I have worked for you and how your cattle were taken care of by me. 30 The little you had before I came has increased into a multitude, and the Lord has blessed you since my arrival; and now, when may I provide for my own household?" 31 And he said, "What shall I give you?" And Jacob said, "Don't give me anything, and if you will do this for me, I will go on feeding and keeping your flock: 32 I will pass through all your flock today and remove from them all the speckled and spotted cattle, and all the brown stock among the sheep, and the spotted and speckled among the goats, and they will be my wages. 33 And my honesty will testify for me in time to come, when you will come to check on the

wages you have paid me. Any goat that is not speckled and spotted, and brown among the sheep, will be considered stolen by me." 34 And Laban said, "Behold, let it be as you have said." 35 And he removed that day all the male goats that were ring-streaked and spotted, and all the female goats that were speckled and spotted, and everyone that had some white in it, and all the brown among the sheep, and he placed them into the hands of his sons. 36 And he set three days journey between himself and Jacob, and Jacob fed the rest of Laban's flocks. 37 And Jacob took him fresh-cut branches from poplar, and of the hazel and chestnut tree, and made white streaks in them by exposing the white inner wood of the branches. 38 And he set the peeled branches before the flocks in the gutters in the watering troughs when the flocks came to drink, that they should conceive when they came to drink. 39 And the flocks conceived before the branches, and brought forth cattle ring-streaked, speckled, and spotted. 40 And Jacob separated the lambs and set the faces of the flocks toward the ring-streaked, and all the brown in the flock of Laban; and he put his own flocks by themselves and put them not with Laban's cattle. 41 And it came to pass that whenever the stronger females did conceive, that Jacob would place the branches in the gutters in front of the eyes of the cattle so they might conceive among the rods. 42 But when the cattle were feeble, he would not place them there. So the feebler

were Laban's and the stronger were Jacob's. 43 And the man grew exceedingly prosperous and had much cattle, and maidservants and menservants, and camels and asses.

The Origins of the Universe

Jacob was ready to leave Laban after Joseph was born. This is a beautiful and revealing part of the Bible. Why should we listen to this story about sheep and cattle with speckles, spots, and streaks?

Rav Ashlag explains that the words *akudim, nekudim, uvrudim* (streaked, speckled, and spotted), refer to the origins of Creation, not the origins of the body. They refer to that first moment in time, when everything emerged from nothingness, and before it became manifested in a physical nature. We are discussing a time long before the stem cell. We have an opportunity with this portion to return to a time before Creation itself. Nowhere but in the Book of Beresheet are we given a chance such as this.

To go back to before the physical reality manifested, and with our consciousness acting like anti-matter, which is also known as Chesed or "water," we are imbued with compassion, sensitivity, and a little caring for others. There are those who say they do not want to share, but in the end, only one with the sharing consciousness—one such as Jacob—will reap all the benefits available. Jealousy is looking at what others have and at what we do not have. This attitude has no place in sharing. In fact, I would suggest to those who possess the consciousness of jealousy, not to bother with Kabbalah at all because it does not work under such conditions.

Streaked, Speckled, and Spotted: Secrets of Creation

This story is probably the most significant part of this biblical section. After all the enormous wealth that was obtained by Jacob and his father-in-law, Jacob wanted to move on with his wives and children, but first they needed to divide the wealth. Jacob told Laban that he would take the speckled, streaked, and spotted newborn animals and leave the rest to Laban.

I love this section, yet it does not really make sense. But the most powerful energy is revealed here. Without going into the full meaning of the spotted, speckled, and streaked markings, this story contains all the secrets of the universe, all the structures of how the world was formed. The procedure relating to how Creation takes place every day anew on the physical level is here in this portion. There are always new things emerging right here by these three words: spotted, speckled, and streaked. We can absorb the knowledge of how we can manipulate the entire structure of the universe for our own benefit, so that it does not create chaos. We have this tremendous opportunity given to us through these three words—*akudim, nekudim, uvrudim*—to influence our entire destiny, improving and correcting it.

One of the most difficult tasks that lie before astrophysicists is that they want to return to the origin of the Universe, the Big Bang. It is not as difficult as it may seem, though. Kabbalists know what caused the Big Bang—it was the TzimTzum, the First Restriction. However, science has not yet arrived at this truth. Science knows what happened mere seconds after the Big Bang. What will happen when they can look beyond that moment? Will they then truly understand what emerged? It is only at the root that one can start really affecting change. Those who believe they can touch the root of their own stem cells, as we do in the Keter of the Musaf Connection, we are able to regenerate different parts of the body that have become weakened. We can return back to the level from whence all our problems originate and, instead, attain there the rejuvenation of existence in our bodies. If we cannot go back, then all we can do is what science has left us with, which is to attempt to cut out the cancer or the problem. If we can go back to the Keter level, we can rejuvenate ourselves and create new cells. Whenever science grasps the energy of such ideas, it is due to a connection with the work we do at The Kabbalah Centre. Whenever we introduce new ways of looking at things, people invariably criticize us. They ask why we do not just leave things the way they are. We may only be a handful of people, but we say no to the world's chaos, and we will always strive to make things better.

Beresheet 31:1 And he heard the words of Laban's sons saying, "Jacob has taken away all that was our fathers and of that which was our fathers has he gained all this wealth." 2 And Jacob beheld the countenance of Laban and saw that it was not what it had been before. 3 And the Lord said to Jacob, "Go back to the land of your fathers and to your kindred, and I will be with you." 4 And Jacob sent word to Rachel and Leah to come out to the fields, to his flocks, 5 and said to them, "I see that your father's countenance toward me is not what it was before, but the God of my father has been with me, 6 and you know that I've worked for your father with all my power, 7 and your father has deceived me, and changed my wages ten times, but God has not allowed him to hurt me. 8 If he said, 'The speckled will be your wages,' then all the cattle bore speckled; and if he said, 'The ring-streaked will be your wages,' then bore all the cattle ring-streaked. 9 So God has taken away your father's cattle and given them to me. 10 And it came to pass at the time that the cattle conceived, that I lifted up my eyes and saw in a dream that the rams which leaped upon the cattle were ring-streaked, speckled, and spotted. 11 And the angel of God spoke to me in the dream saying, 'Jacob.' And I said, 'Here I am.' 12 And he said, 'Lift up your eyes and see that all the rams that leap upon the cattle are ring-streaked, speckled, and spotted, for I have seen all that Laban has been doing to you.

13 I am the God of Bethel, where you anointed a pillar and where you made a vow to Me: now arise, leave this land at once and return to the land of your kindred.' " 14 And Rachel and Leah answered and said to him, "Is there still any portion or inheritance for us in our father's house? 15 Does he not regard us as strangers, because he has sold us, and has used up our money? 16 For all the riches that God has taken from our father is ours and our children's now, so do whatever God has told you to do." 17 Then Jacob rose up and put his sons and his wives on camels, 18 and he carried away all his cattle and all his goods he had gotten, the cattle which he got in Paddan Aram, to go to Isaac, his father, in the land of Canaan. 19 And Laban went to shear his sheep and Rachel stole the idols that were her father's. 20 And Jacob stole away without telling Laban the Syrian that he was leaving. 21 So he fled with all that he had, and he rose up and passed over the River, and he headed toward the mount Gilead. 22 And Laban was told on the third day that Jacob had fled. 23 And he took his brethren with him, and pursued Jacob for seven days and caught up with him in the mount of Gilead. 24 And God came to Laban the Syrian in a dream at night and said to him, "Take heed to not say anything to Jacob, either good or bad." 25 Then Laban overtook Jacob. Now Jacob had pitched his tent in the mount, and Laban with his brethren pitched in the mount of Gilead. 26 And Laban said to Jacob, "What have you done?

You have left without me knowing, and carried away my daughters like captives taken with a sword. 27 Why did you run off secretly and steal away from me, and not tell me, so that I could send you away with joy and with songs, with tambourines and with harps? 28 And not allowed me to kiss my sons and my daughters? You have done a foolish thing. 29 It is in the power of my hand to hurt you; but the God of your father said to me last night, 'Take heed not to say anything to Jacob, either good or bad.' 30 And now, though you desire to be gone because you longed to return to your father's house, yet why did you steal my gods?" 31 Jacob answered and said to Laban, "Because I was afraid, for I said that you might take your daughters away from me by force. 32 With whoever you find your gods, let him not live: Before our brethren, discern for yourself what is yours with me; and take it to yourself." For Jacob knew not that Rachel had stolen them. 33 And Laban went into Jacob's tent and into Leah's tent and into the tent of the two maidservants, but he found nothing. Then he went out of Leah's tent, and entered into Rachel's tent. 34 Now Rachel had taken the idols and put them inside her camel's saddle and sat upon them. And Laban searched the whole tent but found no idols. 35 And she said to her father, "Let it not upset my lord that I cannot rise before you, for the custom of women is upon me." And he searched but could not find the idols. 36 And Jacob was angry and took Laban to task, and Jacob said to Laban, "What is my crime, what is my sin, that you have pursued me so hotly? 37 Now that you have searched all my goods, what have you found of your household stuff? Put it here in front of my brethren and your brethren so that they may judge between the two of us. 38 For the twenty years I have been with you, your ewes and your she-goats have not miscarried, and I have not eaten the rams of your flock. 39 I did not bring you the animals torn by wild beasts; I bore the loss myself. And you required payment from me for whatever was stolen by day or night. 40 This was my situation: in the day the drought consumed me and the frost by night, and my sleep departed from my eyes. 41 For the twenty years I was in your household I worked for you fourteen years for your two daughters and six years for your flocks, and you changed my wages ten times. 42 If the God of my father, the God of Abraham and the Fear of Isaac had not been with me, you would surely have sent me away empty-handed. But God has seen my hardship and the toil of my hands, and rebuked you last night." 43 And Laban answered and said to Jacob, "These daughters are my daughters, and these children are my children, and these cattle are my cattle, and all you see is mine. Yet what can I do today about these daughters of mine, or about the children they have borne? 44 Now therefore, come let us make a covenant, you and I, and let it serve as a witness between us." 45 And

Jacob took a stone and set it up as a pillar. 46 And Jacob said to his brethren, "Gather stones." And they took stones and piled them in a heap, and they ate there on the heap. 47 And Laban called it Jegar Sahadutha, and Jacob called it Galeed. 48 And Laban said, "This heap is a witness between you and me this day." That is why it was called Galeed, 49 and Mizpah, because he said, "May the Lord keep watch between you and me when we are away from each other. 50 If you shall mistreat my daughters or if you take other wives besides my daughters, no man is with us, God is a witness between you and me." 51 And Laban said to Jacob, "Behold this heap, and see this pillar which I have cast between you and me. 52 This heap is a witness, and this pillar is a witness, that I will not go past this heap to you and that you will not go past this heap and pillar to me, to harm. 53 May the God of Abraham and the God of Nahor, the God of their father, judge between us." So Jacob swore by fear in the name of his father Isaac. 54 Then Jacob offered a sacrifice upon the mount and called his relatives to eat bread. And they did eat, and they spent the night there. 55 And early in the morning Laban rose up and kissed his sons and his daughters, and blessed them; and Laban departed and returned to his place.

Beresheet 32:1 Jacob also went on his way, and the angels of God met him. 2 When

Jacob saw them, he said, "This is the camp of God!" So he named that place Mahanaim.

Laban and Satan

If there was any story I could choose to destroy someone's confidence and faith in the Bible, this is the story. It is also the one that I most love. What kind of idiot was I before Kabbalah? This story is about "I want." It tells us to look to Laban, Jacob's father-in-law, who was the epitome of that entity that creates the illusion of time, space, and motion—he is a manifestation of Satan. Satan is immaterial but he has those who appear on a physical level, such as Laban.

This was one of the things that amazed me when I came to Kabbalah: The Zohar gleaned from information in the Bible that it was discussing the creation of the universe on different levels. The real meaning of these stories is so concealed, for how can Creation be related to this story of Laban and Jacob? So often those who merely read the translations dismiss it out of hand. Is Jacob simply teaching us how to trick someone, which is what we can derive from the literal translation? The Bible is speaking about connecting to the levels of consciousness in different created worlds and how, when we pray, we want to elevate our consciousness so that we see things as they are. The Zohar says we have an opportunity to go back to the moment before the beginning of Creation. Changing what exists can be difficult but with experience we can change things even after they have already manifested in the physical world. It is understandable that those who still have ego might not want to accept this.

The universe is a dangerous place, especially today, because of the unfortunate circumstances that most, if not all, of humankind has to endure. I have found what is revealed in this portion to be the most difficult proposition that we can attempt to place into our consciousness and truly believe. Science says the physical reality is an illusionary blip on the screen, and this theory has been validated. The physical reality exists to cause us problems. The physical body—with its cancer, headaches, and stomach upsets and so on—is a never-ending source of misery and distraction. And beyond the body, we struggle with the physical realities of finances and daily life. Science says that which is not in our consciousness is not reality. Even other people are an illusionary reality. A person is not measured by his physical stature; a brilliant man is not necessarily someone who is handsome or intelligent. Says the Zohar, 2,000 years ago, we are what we think. Those who are unwilling to begin to infuse their consciousness with this idea are not suited to the study of Kabbalah. Those who do not connect with the weekly reading and do not understand the words, and have not truly heard the reading on Shabbat, have no chance of escaping chaos that coming week. We should never miss the reading because this much is guaranteed: those who do not listen to the reading do not escape chaos. This is what the Zohar says, and I have found it to be true.

BOOK OF BERESHEET:

Portion of Vayishlach

PORTION OF VAYISHLACH

**Beresheet 32:3 Jacob sent messengers ahead
of him to his brother Esau in the land of Seir,
the country of Edom. 4 He instructed them:
"This is what you are to say to my master
Esau: 'Your servant Jacob says, I have been
staying with Laban and have remained there
till now. 5 I have cattle and donkeys, sheep
and goats, menservants and maidservants.
Now I am sending this message to my lord,
that I may find favor in your eyes.'"**

Jacob Sent Messengers to Esau

In these passages we see a confrontation between Jacob and Esau.
After being separated from his brother for 22 years, Jacob was faced
with his brother advancing towards him supported by four hundred
men. There are many interpretations concerning the identity of the
messengers sent by Jacob. Rashi states that they were angels; others
say they were human beings. The Zohar says:

> "And Jacob sent messengers..." (Beresheet 32:3) Rav Yehuda
> began the discussion with the verse, "For He shall give
> His angels charge over you, to keep you in all your ways."
> (Tehilim 91:11) This verse has already been explained by
> the friends. When man is born, the Evil Inclination enters
> with him and constantly denounces him, as it is written,
> "sin crouches at the door." (Beresheet 4:7) What is meant
> by "sin crouches"? It refers to the Evil Inclination. "...at
> the door" means at the opening of the womb at a person's
> birth... The Evil Inclination never leaves man, from the day

of his birth. The Good Inclination comes to man only when he seeks purity. And when does man seek purity? On his thirteenth birthday, man joins with the Good Inclination on the Right and the Evil Inclination on the Left. They are literally two appointed angels found constantly with man.
—Zohar, Vayishlach 1:1-3

Jacob was a human being. What does scripture mean by saying that he sent angels to Esau? How did Jacob control angels? Are they not on a higher level than a man or woman?

The Zohar explains that the sending of angels is really about consciousness. When Jacob dispatched the angels, he was preparing himself for war. How do we prepare for war on a physical level? Do we just send troops into battle? No, we plan and strategize at an army headquarters. First there has to be a strategy—and by "strategy" we mean consciousness. Is the battle between Esau and Jacob a physical war? The Zohar says no. Moreover, the Zohar takes it one step further, saying that all wars are fought with consciousness.

The battle between Jacob and Esau is not, as many interpret it to be, a war between the Jew and the non-Jew. This is the way it is traditionally viewed, though, because Esau is considered to be the father of the non-Jewish nations. The Zohar says something different, however. It explains that the battle between Jacob and Esau is the battle that each one of us faces every single day—the battle of uncertainty, the battle with a spouse, the battle with co-workers or friends, and so on. It is not a battle between Jew and non-Jew because if every person in general, and the Jews in particular, could straighten out their own lives, according to the Zohar, the whole world would be straightened out. The battle described in the Bible is not referring to battlefields or to people of differing faiths, it is discussing the two types of consciousness—the

Desire to Share and the Desire to Receive—that exist within every individual. This is the battle that everyone is faced with throughout our lives. If a person is negative in nature, that person will conduct his business, even his relationship with his family in a negative way; and the opposite is also true for those of a positive nature. What the Zohar means by angels is really what is happening inside of us. Angels are not those beautiful depictions of winged beings familiar from so many stories; angels are consciousness. The Zohar continues:

> Rav Elazar applies this verse to Jacob. As the Holy One, blessed be He, surrounded Jacob with legions of angels because he came complete with the Supernal tribes, who were in a state of perfection. As it is written, "And Jacob continued on his way, and angels of God met him." (Beresheet 32:2) It has been explained that after being saved from Laban, and departing from him, the Shechinah joined Jacob, and legions of saintly angels surrounded him. At that point "Jacob said when he saw them." (Ibid. 3) From these angels, he sent a group to Esau. This is the meaning of the verse, "And Jacob sent messengers (also: angels)." Surely these were real angels.
> —Zohar, Vayishlach 1: 5

When an individual is thinking in terms of sharing and receiving, he or she is in a circuit of energy because there is a balance between the two. And when a person is in balance, these two aspects of consciousness will watch over him. Nothing and no one will ever be able to touch him. This is what is being discussed here.

On the superficial level, Esau certainly came to destroy Jacob. But Jacob was already looking within to see if he himself was complete. He knew that if he was complete, then he had nothing to fear. Being complete depends on whether the two aspects of consciousness—the Desire to Receive and the Desire to Share—are in balance. Being able to think and reflect within becomes an opportunity rather than something chaotic. The battle was not going to take place when he met Esau. The war was conducted long before the meeting because the battle was an introspective, spiritual struggle.

When the messengers returned to Jacob, they informed him that they had met his brother Esau, who was now approaching, meaning Esau did not accept the gifts.

The Zohar says:

> "And Jacob sent messengers." Rav Aba asks, "What motivated Jacob TO SEND MESSENGERS to Esau? Would it not have been better to refrain from sending any to him?" He answers, "Jacob said, 'I know that Esau reveres our father's honor and has never troubled him. As long as I know that my father is alive, so I do not fear Esau. So as long as my father is alive I wish to appease him.' Thus he immediately HASTENED, 'and Jacob sent messengers before him.'"
> —Zohar, Vayishlach 1:15

Esau thought Jacob had stolen the birthright. And, even from the point of view of scripture, it appears as if Jacob had indeed tricked Isaac over the birthright. And this incident shows that Esau was certainly not Jacob's friend. In fact, Esau said that the moment his father Isaac leaves this world, he would then come to kill Jacob. For this reason, Rav Aba, in the Zohar, asks why Jacob sends messengers to Esau. Would it not be better for Jacob to remain silent, so that Esau would not know his whereabouts? There would also then be less possibility for negativity to be aroused. The Zohar answers that Esau was fearful about compromising the honor of their venerable father, and he would thus never do anything to anger or shame

Isaac. So Jacob had nothing to fear from him while their father was still alive, and perhaps he could in some way encourage Esau to forgive him. What is the Zohar revealing here?

The Zohar is teaching us how we must conduct ourselves. When Rav Aba said it would be better if Jacob had kept silent, did it mean that it is better not to rock the boat and to leave things as they are? Maybe the unresolved issues will go away? The biblical text makes it sound as if Jacob was behaving as though nothing had happened between him and his brother. But the Zohar is here providing the answer alongside the question. Rav Aba knew that the Bible tells us Esau would do nothing to harm Jacob as long as Isaac was alive, nevertheless his question remained. Perhaps it would simply go away? Perhaps Jacob's strategy would work, giving him more time? However, what the Zohar says is that the problem with Esau would not go away, teaching us that problems do not simply disappear, do not just go away. We may wish for the conflicts in our lives to disappear. We may even tell ourselves that we will deal with them tomorrow but, according to the Zohar, everything has to be addressed. We have all heard the expression "time heals" or we may have said ourselves to "give it some time;" but the Zohar says that problems left to themselves will never go away, no matter how much time passes. Whatever comes up has to be dealt with. The Zohar does not tell us how problems should be dealt with but rather it says that things will not go away by themselves. Jacob felt that the problem would not go away and would, therefore, have to be managed somehow.

The Zohar continues:

> Rav Shimon began the discussion with the verse, "Better is one lightly esteemed who owns a servant, than one who pranks himself but lacks bread." (Mishlei 12:9) This verse refers to the Evil Inclination, who constantly accuses man.

The Evil Inclination causes man to become haughty and proud, encouraging man to curl his hair until the Evil Inclination towers over him and drags him to Gehenom. "Better is one lightly esteemed" means one who does not follow the Evil Inclination, and does not act haughtily but humbles his spirit, heart, and will before the Holy One, blessed be He. Then the Evil Inclination becomes his servant, as it cannot control him. ON THE CONTRARY, the person controls it, as it is written, "Yet you may rule over him." (Beresheet 4:7) "…than one who pranks himself" is as we said, that he puts on airs, curls his hair, and acts haughtily, "but lacks bread," THIS MEANS a lack of faith, as it is written, "to offer the bread of his God," (Vayikra 21:17) and "the bread of their God they do offer." (Ibid. 6) BREAD IS THE SCHECHINAH IN BOTH VERSES. FAITH IS THE SHECHINAH, SO LACKING BREAD MEANS LACKING FAITH.

Another interpretation of, "Better is one lightly esteemed" is that it refers to Jacob, who humbled himself before Esau so that Esau should later become his servant. By controlling him, he fulfilled the meaning of the verse, "Let peoples serve you, and nations bow down to you." (Beresheet 27:29) It was not yet time FOR JACOB TO RULE OVER ESAU. Jacob left this to happen at a later time, for he was lowly then. Later, however, the one who pranks himself will become his servant, and then he will "lack bread." THIS REFERS TO ESAU, who will become JACOB'S servant, who was given "plenty of corn and wine." (Ibid. 28)

Come and behold, Jacob knew that he needed him now. Therefore, he appeared as if he was lightly esteemed. By doing so, he showed more wisdom and guile than he had ever shown against Esau. Had Esau been aware of this wisdom, he would have killed himself rather than coming to this. However, Jacob did all this with wisdom, and about him Hannah said, "The adversaries of the Lord shall be broken in pieces and He shall give strength to his king." (I Shmuel 2:10)

—Zohar, Vayishlach 1:16-20

What does it mean to go after the Evil Inclination? Jacob did not experience any ego. He directed his thoughts and his heart only to God, meaning he understood that he was incompetent and could not do anything, and that if God would help him then everything would work out for the best. The Zohar explains that if a person thinks along these lines, the Evil Inclination, Satan or chaos becomes a slave to him. When a person restricts the ego, suppresses it and has no ego at all, then the Evil Inclination, which is chaos, cannot touch them. If we are totally involved with the Lightforce, then there cannot be chaos. Many of us have an excess of pride: "See how smart I am? See how much I understand?" But, even with all our wisdom, if we possess it, in one minute that wisdom can disappear. This story teaches us not only that a person must not have pride, but also that, when a person resists his or her own ego and has no evil inclination, then chaos cannot touch them. On the contrary, such a person rules over the evil inclination.

What is pride to God? "God reigned and was clothed in pride" (Tehilim 93:1) is a verse of scripture we recite on Fridays, and which seems to say that the Creator has pride, meaning that God is involved with ego. The reality, however, is that the power of the Lightforce of the Creator is the opposite of chaos. If one is totally involved with the Light, there can be no chaos. When a person wants to say who he is and how smart he is and how wise, everyone can see that he is intelligent but does he have *control* along with all his wisdom and knowledge? Is he in charge? No. Because anything at all can happen in a second, God forbid! But with the power of

Light nothing chaotic can occur. When we are involved with the Lightforce, when we are really with the Lightforce, then we know we are really in control of anything and everything—there is no question about it. If we feel that we are with the Lightforce then we understand that it is not us and, therefore, *ge'ut* (I am in control) is appropriate.

6 When the messengers returned to Jacob, they said, "We went to your brother Esau, and now he is coming to meet you, and four hundred men are with him."

Prayers of the Righteous

The Zohar says:

> The messengers returned to Jacob, saying: "We went to your brother Esau, and now he is coming to meet you, and four hundred men with him." (Beresheet 32:7) HE ASKS, "After saying, 'We came to your brother,' do we not know they referred to Esau, as he had no other brothers?" HE ANSWERS,"We came to your brother" MEANS THAT he did not repent and walk the path of righteousness, as may be thought, but remained the evil Esau as before. "…and he is also coming to meet you…" does not mean, as you may say, by himself, but rather he has "four hundred men with him."
>
> Why was all this specified? Because the Holy One, blessed be He, always longs for the prayers of the righteous and adorns Himself with them. As we have already said, the angel in charge of the prayers of Israel, whose name is Sandalfon, receives all their prayers and weaves them into a crown for the Life of the Worlds. The Holy One, blessed be He, desires the prayers of the righteous all the more; they become a crown with which to adorn the Holy One, blessed be He. You may wonder why Jacob was fearful, since camps of Holy angels accompanied him. He was fearful because the righteous do not rely on their merit, but on their prayers and supplications before their Master.
> —Zohar, Vayishlach 3:43-44

It is an aspect of human nature to believe that things are true when they are not at all true. We like to rationalize irrationality. When we want something desperately enough, we can turn the object of our desire it into a white lie. We justify and rationalize to give ourselves permission to do whatever it is we yearn for or crave. We find all the reasons that exist for why we are completely right in our actions. This is our ego at work—the ego which can be summed up by one word: ME. Everything is for, and about, me—that is the thinking. If everyone considered us to be a great person, then we would receive respect, honor or whatever it is we want in the way of praise. We thus want to have an ego because we imagine it is only in this way that we will receive what we desire.

Why did Jacob think that Esau had repented? The Zohar asks why Jacob underwent the process of sending Esau presents and of praying to God. There is a tremendous lesson for us all here, especially in our present times. Can two brothers who did not care for each other begin to care and effect this transformation almost overnight, too? A person who truly repents is someone who has changed internally; it is not someone who has merely altered his or her external appearance and behavior. Therefore, Esau remained the same internally as he always had been. So the Zohar asks why Jacob sent him gifts and prayed to God. Jacob is one of the Chariots, a portal of the Central Column; and the man able to balance the Right with the Left can, by doing so, control the whole world. Nothing can touch the individual able to create a totality of balance between Right and Left. No matter what is happening to everyone else around him, he will be totally unaffected by it.

The Zohar says that the Lord desires the prayers of the righteous. Does this mean we must all become totally religious people who fulfill the precepts because God has commanded us to do so? No. The Zohar is not of the opinion that what we do here is for God because this would then imply that God is missing something, that we are meant to fulfill His desires and wishes. What we are meant to understand from this story is not how to fulfill God's wishes but rather how we can develop ourselves internally—nothing more, nothing less.

The Lightforce of God lacks for absolutely nothing. The Lightforce is the all-embracing unified whole, complete and entire. However, even when we do not have a lack or a need of anything, we can still receive. There is no such thing as someone who cannot be a recipient of sharing, and there is a story to illustrate this concept. A rich man invited a poor man to his home for a meal, urging the man to please help himself to all the food he wanted. To this, the poor man replied, "I'm not hungry but, even if I were hungry, who is to say that I need any favors from you?" The rich man continued to plead with the poor man, "Please, please eat." The poor man finally said, "Well, if it means so much to you, I'll eat." The wealthy man was fully taken care of physically, emotionally, and mentally. However, this did not preclude him from receiving. With each bite of food the poor man ate, he imparted and shared with the rich man.

This is what the Zohar means when it says that the *tzadikim* (righteous souls) crown the Creator. The Creator created everything for our benefit. If we were to refuse His beneficence, while this would not cause a lack in the Creator, it would also not result in circuitry. The purpose of God creating everything is so that we can participate in His sharing. And when we accept His sharing, as the poor man accepted the sustenance given by the rich man, we create a circle of energy that can flow unimpeded. A righteous person understands that with every interaction there must be a sharing and a receiving at the same time. While the poor man needed food, his receiving at the same time gave pleasure to the rich man, who was now able to share his food, and in this way the poor man was also sharing. Although the rich man was the giver, he too was receiving from the poor man, who agreed to accept his gifts. This interaction is a complete interaction, for any interaction that does not consist of both aspects—receiving and sharing—is not complete.

In this universe, the reality and paradox of polarity always exists. When we have both polarities operating at the same time, then we have reality. Without the opposites of positive and negative working together, we do not have reality, instead we have illusion. Even in the light bulb it is only opposites—a positive and a negative pole—that together create the light. When there is light, there is reality, and this reality only exists because both polarities are present. We make both present at the same time through the aspect of Restriction, of balance. This is what the Zohar means here, and why the Lord desires the prayers of the righteous. The Zohar says:

> Come and behold, Rav Shimon said that the prayer of the congregation rises before the Holy One, blessed be He, and He is adorned by that prayer because it ascends in several ways, ONE ASKING FOR CHASADIM, ANOTHER FOR GEVUROT, AND A THIRD FOR MERCY. IT consists of several sides, THE RIGHT SIDE, THE LEFT, AND THE MIDDLE, AS CHASADIM ARE DRAWN FORM THE RIGHT, GEVUROT FROM THE LEFT, AND MERCY FORM THE MIDDLE. Because it comprises several aspects, it is woven into a wreath and put on the head of the Righteous One, the Life of the Worlds THAT IS YESOD, WHICH GIVES SLAVATION TO THE NUKVA AND FORM HER, TO THE WHOLE CONGREGATION. But a solitary prayer does not include all the sides; rather, it contains only one aspect. ONE CAN ONLY ASK FOR CHASADIM, GEVUROT, OR MERCY. Therefore, the solitary prayer is not prepared and accepted as is that of the congregation; IT IS NOT INCLUDED WITHIN ALL THE THREE COLUMNS AS IS THE PRAYER OF THE

CONGREGATION. Come and behold, Jacob included all THREE COLUMNS, BEING THE CHARIOT OF THE CENTRAL COLUMN, WHICH INCLUDES BOTH. Therefore, the Holy One, blessed be He, desired his prayer PERFECTED BY ALL THREE COLUMNS. It is therefore written, "Then Jacob was greatly afraid and distressed." THE HOLY ONE, BLESSED BE HE, DID ALL THAT TO ENCOURAGE JACOB TO PRAY, FOR HE CRAVED HIS PRAYER.
—Zohar, Vayishlach 3:45

The reason for the synagogue (Heb. *Beit haKnesset*) is not that it provides us with a place to pray. We can pray at home. Here, Rav Shimon bar Yochai explains that the reason for a *Beit haKnesset* is because of *tefilat rabim* (the prayer of many)—the positive interaction between the people praying. Yet in many *Beit haKnesset* today, we have lost the essential ingredient of what a *Beit haKnesset* is all about, which is to bring people together into one unified whole. If anything, the *Beit haKnesset* often becomes a place of arguments—even to the extent that people do not talk to each other. How could this have emerged from the original idea of a *Beit haKnesset*?

Therefore, Rav Shimon says the *tefila* (prayer) of a *rabim* (of many) is more important than any other form of *tefila* because he is assuming that the place of a *tefila* exists to bring people together. It is not a place to display the "me," the ego. Rather it is a place where each person should cancel out their individuality and create a *rabim*—and this is the real function of a minyan (ten people gathered together in prayer).

We need ten people because, in this way, we bring together the ten forces that exist in the universe, which are referred to in Kabbalah as the Ten Sefirot. Each individual is represented by a force. A *Beit haKnesset* can be any room; it does not have to be something big or fancy. It is a place where one unified whole forms—a whole made from ten separate individuals. When we have a *Beit haKnesset* of one unified whole, then the *tefila* reaches up and connects with the energy force of God. If this is not what the *Beit haKnesset* is all about, then it is devoid of energy.

God desires the prayers because these ten people make the vessel. When do we share? We share when there is someone to receive from us. These ten people become one unified vessel suitable for asking and receiving. God wants to share more than we want to receive. But if there is no Vessel, then how can He achieve the fulfillment of sharing with us health, serenity, tranquility—everything that we may personally need at the time? Therefore, if this kind of prayer is manifested within a *Beit haKnesset* where there is a *rabim*, then it can most certainly reach the Lord.

Why Four Hundred Men?

Why did Esau come with four hundred men—why not 399 or 401? The number four hundred is much like the four hundred shekels Abraham paid for his land, which are channels of four hundred aspects of metaphysical energy.

7 In great fear and distress Jacob divided the people who were with him into two groups, and the flocks and herds and camels as well. 8 He said, "If Esau comes and attacks one group, the group that is left shall escape." 9 Then Jacob prayed, "God of my father Abraham, God of my father Isaac, Lord, who said to me, 'Go back to your country and your relatives, and I will make you prosper,' 10 I am unworthy of all the kindness and faithfulness you have shown your servant. I had only my staff when I crossed this Jordan, but now I have become two groups. 11 Save me, I pray, from the hand of my brother Esau, for I am afraid he will come and attack me, and also the mothers with their children. 12 But you have said, 'I will surely make you prosper and will make your descendants like the sand of the sea, which cannot be counted.' "

True Fearlessness

Why was Jacob afraid to meet his brother Esau? Jacob was totally connected to God and had nothing to fear. There are two kinds of people who do not have fear: those who are fools because they do not know when to be afraid, and those who are totally connected to the Light.

When we experience fear it is simply a reminder that we need to reconnect with the Lightforce of God, and then the fear will disappear. We should not be alarmed but rather take it as a wake-up call to look to the Light.

13 He spent the night there, and from what he had with him he selected a sacrifice for his brother Esau: 14 two hundred female goats and twenty male goats, two hundred ewes and twenty rams, 15 thirty female camels with their young, forty cows and ten bulls, and twenty female donkeys and ten male donkeys. 16 He put them in the care of his servants, each herd by itself, and said to his servants, "Go ahead of me, and keep some space between the herds." 17 He instructed the one in the lead: "When my brother Esau meets you and asks, 'To whom do you belong, and where are you going, and who owns all these animals in front of you?' 18 then you are to say, 'They belong to your servant Jacob. They are a sacrifice sent to my lord Esau, and he is coming behind us.' " 19 He also instructed the second, the third, and all the others who followed the herds: "You are to say the same thing to Esau when you meet him. 20 And be sure to say, 'Your servant Jacob is coming behind us.' " For he thought, "I will pacify him with these sacrifices I am sending on ahead; later, when I see him, perhaps he will receive me."

Jacob's Sacrifice

The Bible tells us specifically how many oxen and goats Jacob sent as a gift to Esau. It is important we know that Jacob thought he could appease Esau, who was intent on destroying him and his family.

21 So Jacob's sacrifice went on ahead of him, but he himself spent the night in the camp. 22 That night Jacob got up and took his two wives, his two maidservants, and his eleven sons and crossed the ford of the Yabok. 23 After he had sent them across the stream, he sent over all his possessions.

Gathering Every Spark of Light

Jacob went back across the river to fetch some containers he had forgotten on the other side. They could not have been worth more than a few cents, so why did he cross the river to retrieve them? Jacob understood that everything really exists in the form of energy, and so he did not want to miss even one spark of all the energy in the world. Jacob wanted everything. Moreover, if we leave something behind and do not collect it, we are creating an opening for Satan to enter. We need to desire every spark of Light and, when we want everything, it does not matter whether something is very valuable or not.

Yabok and the Names of God

Mathematics is the true language of Kabbalah. The crossing of the river Yabok is mentioned in this section for the purpose of correctly connecting us with the three Names of God, which are *Ehyeh* אהיה, *Tetragrammaton* יהוה, and *Adonai* אדני. According to their numerology, these names together add up to 112, as do the letters of the Hebrew word *yabok*.

24 So Jacob was left alone, and a man wrestled with him till daybreak.

Wrestling the Angel

The English translation of the word *ye'avek* is "wrestled." However, the real meaning is of course much deeper. *Ye'avek* comes from the Hebrew word, *avak*, which means "dust" or "ashes." There are two kinds of dust: the dust of the earth where things can grow, and then the kind of dust resulting when something has been burned—ashes. When something is burned and ashes form, there is no continuity.

This battle between Jacob and the Angel was more than a physical or mental struggle—the Angel of Death was trying to cancel Jacob out completely. This was not to bring about his death, because death would have meant that the Dark Lord overcame the forces of good. *Avak* is so much more than this; it means that he tried to cancel out Jacob to bring an end to continuity. "Ashes" is the perfect choice of word because it expresses an end; we cannot resurrect ashes. This is why, according to Kabbalah, there is to be no cremation for the dead. There is the possibility that the body will be resurrected but with cremation there is no longer any possible continuity. The Bible here is talking about energy-intelligent forces—the power of consciousness.

Were Jacob and this man physically fighting? It says that Jacob was fighting with an angel. An angel is a consciousness, an immortal being, not one clothed in a physical corporeal body. Therefore, this could not be a discussion of physical wrestling (Heb. *he'avkut*) between two physical people. However, this entity could still wrestle, and wrestle with the physical Jacob he did, even causing him an actual physical limp. There is no contradiction in this, for the limp was not a truly physical condition. Today, the medical establishment says that stress is a major cause of disease. Cancer is a person who is eating away at himself because he wants to be free of pain. As Above so Below—this is the rule. Things that appear in the form of stress on a metaphysical or mental level also become manifest on a physical level.

A good analogy for this concept would be water in the form of ice. If the ice has impurities in it, and then we melt the ice, it will take the form of water. And although water and ice look different, the impurities remain—they will not disappear. If we now go one step further and heat the water into steam, dispersing it as molecules, then atoms and so forth, we eventually get to a very pure state—no impurities. The law of as Above so Below, still applies. These substances may not look the same—there is indeed just the illusion that they are not the same—yet atoms, steam, water, and ice are in fact really all the same; we merely do not perceive them as the same.

A major problem today is that we are becoming steadily convinced that our minds are worthless. We are the smartest kingdom (species) in the world, and yet just look at how negative we are about ourselves; so negative that we need the constant assistance of computers and calculators because we cannot do anything by ourselves anymore.

25 When the man saw that he could not over-power him, he touched the socket of Jacob's hip so that his hip was wrenched as he wrestled with him. 26 Then the man said, "Let me go, for it is daybreak." But Jacob replied, "I will not let you go unless you bless me."

The Importance of Time

Why does the Bible make a point of letting us know that Jacob wrestled with the man until daybreak, and at daybreak the man asked Jacob to let him go? What is the importance of us knowing about the time, which was just before dawn? The Zohar says:

> Rav Chiya opened the discussion with the verse, "No evil shall befall you, nor shall any plague come near your dwelling." (Tehilim 91:10) Come and behold, when the Holy One, blessed be He, created the world, He performed in each day the work appropriate for that day, as has been explained. It has been said that on the Fourth Day He created the lights, but the moon was created lacking, because it is a light that diminishes itself. For that reason, the word "lights" is spelled without the letter *Vav*, which leaves room for the spirits, demons, storm winds, devils, and all the Spirits of Defilement to exercise sway.

> Rav Elazar said, "Man has been warned not to venture out alone at night, especially when the moon was created lacking, AND DOES NOT FULLY SHINE. It has been explained that the Spirit of Defilement, an evil spirit, governs at that time."
> —Zohar, Vayishlach 4:75 & 80

The Zohar explains that we are talking about cosmic energy-intelligences. The sun never rises and it never sets. But, insofar as we are concerned, it appears as if the sun rises and sets. The sun is shining in the Philippines, while it is nighttime in New York. The Zohar says that when nightfall comes, there is a new cosmic ruler, and this ruler of negativity reigns until the appearance of the morning star or dawn.

Now, thanks to the Bible, we have a timetable. It is wonderful for us to do our thing whenever we like—even for those of us on a spiritual path. However, if we are not aware of the timetable, if we are not aware of the cosmic forces all around us, we cannot possibly rule in this domain. And this is in spite of how strong we are in internalizing this wisdom, regardless of how much we study, or how frequently we do all the good and right things. These things simply do not count if we are ignorant of the timetable.

It is vital we know that there are timetables. Morning means one thing, and afternoon means another—this is what the Bible is telling us here. Therefore, kabbalistically speaking, just as there is a different meditation for every sign of the zodiac, there is also a meditation for the three periods of a 24-hour day. There are also different prayers for Pesach, Shavuot, Sukkot, Rosh Hashanah, and Yom Kippur, which are other cosmic events taking place that we can also connect to and that we should all be aware of.

The angel wanted to be sent away at dawn because Jacob had now taken total control. But if Jacob had control and he now overpowered the seed—the DNA structure of all evil and negativity in the world—why should he send him away? He could have simply finished the job, making it easier for the rest of us. The Zohar explains that this is the precise reason he had to send the man away. Even though Jacob took control of this period from dusk until the dawn, what about all the souls that have to return for their *tikkun* (spiritual correction) and consequently must have the free choice between doing good or evil? The only way we can work out our correction is by living in the mud and muck of life.

If we are living only within a spiritual frame of reference where it is beautiful, no one is bothering us, and we are connected with God, then we are also moving ahead to nowhere. There cannot be a performance and completion of *tikkun* under such circumstances. This is why the wrestling angel said, "Send me away." But what we learn here is that we can take control, that the negative force will no longer rule over us because we can tell him, if we know how—and we have the knowledge now to do this. Why does the kabbalist get up in middle of the night and study until dawn? He or she knows the timetable. It is not that they are religious, or pious, or even studious people. They simply know when the cosmic Lightforce is prevalent, know that the most purified time in the cosmos is from midnight until the rising of the morning star. This is when we can make connections and instill within ourselves the Central Column force, which is the quintessential balance (represented here by Jacob). The Zohar assures us that if we have this internal balance, there is no outside chaos in this world that can affect us.

**27 He asked him, "What is your name?"
"Jacob," he answered. 28 Then he said, "Your
name will no longer be Jacob, but Israel, because you have struggled with God and with
men and have overcome." 29 Jacob said,
"Please tell me your name." But he replied,
"Why do you ask my name?" And he blessed
him there. 30 So Jacob called the place Peniel,
saying, "It is because I saw God face to face,
and yet my life was spared." 31 The sun rose
above him as he passed Peniel, and he was
limping because of his hip. 32 Therefore, to
this day the Israelites do not eat the sciatic
nerve attached to the socket of the hip, because the socket of Jacob's hip was touched
near that sinew.**

The Meaning of the Name "Israel"

As Rashi and the Zohar both state, Jacob remained alone because
he had forgotten some small jars on the other side of the river, and
then he wrestled with an angel until dawn. The angel wounded him
in the inner thigh and said, "From now on your name is 'Israel'."

At the end of this portion, it states that God saw Jacob, blessed him,
and told him that his name would no longer be "Jacob"—that he
would now be called "Israel." How are we to understand that the
Creator of the universe said this? Then who was it really that gave
Jacob the name "Israel"?

The Zohar says:

> "And there wrestled a man with him." HE ASKS, "What
> does 'wrestled' (Heb. *veya'avek*) mean?" Rav Shimon replies,
> "HE CAME TO HIM from the dust (Heb. *avak*), AS
> SHALL BE EXPLAINED. Dust is of lesser importance
> than earth." HE ASKS, "What is the difference between
> dust and earth?" HE ANSWERS, "Dust is the residue of
> fire, that is, WHAT IS LEFT FROM FIRE IS CALLED
> 'DUST.' It never produces fruits. From earth, however, all
> fruits grow, as it comprises everything Above and Below."

> Rav Yehuda said, "If this is so, AND EARTH IS OF SUCH
> CONSEQUENCE, then what is THE MEANING OF
> THE VERSE, 'He raises the poor out of the dust (lit.
> "earth")'?" (I Shmuel 2:8) He replies, "Literally, IT MEANS
> 'HUMILITY.' In such a way He raises the poor out of the
> earth because THE NUKVA CALLED 'EARTH,' has
> nothing of her own BUT RECEIVES EVERYTHING
> FROM ZEIR ANPIN. Then out of the earth, WHICH
> POSSESSES NOTHING AS LONG AS IT IS NOT
> UNITED WITH ZEIR ANPIN, come the poor, who
> possess nothing. But out of earth, AT THE TIME OF
> UNION WITH ZEIR ANPIN, come all the fruits and
> goodness of the world. All that is done in the world is made
> from the earth, as it is written, 'All are of the earth, and all
> return to earth.'" (Kohelet 3:20) We have learned that all
> is of the earth, even the wheel of the Sun, but dust never
> produces fruits and plants. Therefore, "there wrestled a
> man," SAMAEL, who came out of the dust, HIS NUKVA,
> and rides upon it to accuse Jacob.

> "...until the breaking of the day..." is the time when his power
> goes away and disappears, as will occur in the future. For the

exile resembles the night; NAMELY IT IS DARK, a time when the dust rules over Israel, and the people are thrown to the earth until light appears and daylight shines. Then Israel will have power and will be given the Kingdom, for they will be high saints, as it is written, "And the kingdom and dominion, and the greatness of the kingdoms under the whole Heaven, shall be given to the people of the Holy Ones of the most High, whose Kingdom is an everlasting Kingdom, and all dominions shall serve and obey Him." (Daniel 7:27)
—Zohar, Vayishlach 5:87-89

When the Zohar states that from dust there is no continuity, it means that the angel knew he was no longer in control; and this is why he says "now that the morning star has risen, I have to go." Exile is like the night or darkness, and when day will come, the Israelites will go out of exile. Exile is equated with dust and chaos. Chaos is anything that comes to an abrupt end. We are born with health but it comes to an end. We earn a living, and it also comes to an end. This is all considered to be the realm where the *avak* (dust) rules.

From the Zohar it is clear that when Jacob wrestled with the angel, he was wrestling with chaos. When the angel told Jacob that his name would now be "Israel," it was to inform him that he was now connected to the Tree of Life, where discontinuity, chaos or Satan have no dominion. The angel's blessing was that all the Israelites would ultimately achieve the spiritual level of Israel—the Tree of Life Reality. The angel blessed Jacob so that he could move out of the realm of chaos—the Lower Triad, which is the name "Jacob"—and elevate into the Upper Triad of "Israel."

The reason why Jacob wanted the angel to bless him was not for the blessing itself, but rather it was because the angel was the metaphysical counterpart of Esau. The Zohar says that Jacob wanted the angel to agree that the blessing of the birthright Isaac had given Jacob did indeed belong to him. Esau never admitted that he had sold Jacob the birthright, instead he accused Jacob of stealing it from him. This is why Jacob asked the angel to bless him. The reason Jacob said that he would not send the angel away is to show us that even in *galut* (exile) we can have dominion over Satan. The blessing of the angel was not about giving Jacob the name of "Israel" but rather the angel's blessing was about Esau. This is why God blessed Jacob with the name of Israel later in this portion.

Jacob Wrestles with the Angel—Esau's Energetic Counterpart

Jacob fell asleep alone in this place, and he wrestled with a man in his dream until the rise of the morning star. At the end of their struggle the man blessed him. The Zohar says that the Bible is not telling us a story to waste our time but rather that there are two things at work: Jacob's dream and the manifestation of that dream with the physical encounter of Jacob and Esau. The dream Jacob had described the struggle with Esau in the metaphysical realm. It represents the consciousness before a battle begins—the time when we formulate a plan in our mind. Why do we begin to hate someone? Where does the hatred come from? It starts with the mind, with rationalization. Before the manifestation of hate, we formulate a thought or perception in our mind. Something does not become manifest physically unless it is first formulated in our consciousness. In other words, confrontation does not begin at the physical level.

The Zohar further explains that the wrestling that took place is referring to the snake, which represents evil as it exists in this physical world. Evil is part of the landscape of this planet, and it has to be eliminated. If there are evil thoughts, it is because evil is an energy that exists here. We intrinsically justify an evil that is not of our creation. At this point in the story, the morning star appears; and the morning star indicates the darkest point of the day—the time just before nightfall and daybreak come together. It is when night ends and the sun rises. It is darkest at that time, when the line of blackness is so distinct from the light.

The kabbalist is up at this time; he or she wakes up to draw down the Lightforce to give themselves a chance of survival. The moment of the rising of the morning star is when we can overcome evil for the coming day. At this moment we study Torah and other meditations that Rav Isaac Luria (the Ari, 1534 – 1573) provided, formulae that remove every aspect of chaos.

At this point in the story, Satan gave Jacob a new name, "Israel," and later God gave him the name "Israel" as well. We work to raise our consciousness to connect to the level of Israel, the realm where no chaos at all comes down. When we are clothed in our negativity, chaos is still present and we question where God is. Israel is a level of consciousness, a place in this universe where chaos does not exist in any form. Some chaos is irrevocable, some chaos is not. The dialogue between Jacob and the angel of Esau, in Jacob's dream, is all about how we can remove the extreme chaos from our lives—just as Jacob did.

The Sciatic Nerve

After wrestling with the angel, in the early morning, Jacob found that he was limping. The Zohar says:

> "Therefore the children of Israel eat not of the sinew of the vein because he touched the hollow of Jacob's thigh in the sinew of the vein." It is forbidden to enjoy it or even to

give it to a dog. HE ASKS, "Why is it called the 'sinew of the vein' (Heb. *nashe*)?" HE ANSWERS, "The sinew SEDUCES (Heb. *menasheh*) men from serving their Master. There lies the Evil Inclination. When the angel wrestled with Jacob, he could not find a weak place in his body through which to overcome Jacob, because the parts of his body were all strong and without weakness; AND THE KLIPA TAKES HOLD ONLY IN A PLACE OF WANT AND WEAKNESS. What did he do then? 'He touched the hollow of his thigh,' the sinew of the vein, his own kind, that is, the Evil Inclination which is his own kind. And there is the place OF THE EVIL INCLINATION. from where it comes to harm people."

For that reason the Torah reads, "Therefore the children of Israel eat not of the sinew of the vein." The friends said that a man's body parts allude to higher places. IF THE MEMBER is good, IT DRAWS goodness; if it be evil, it draws evil. Thus, each animal member we eat strengthens the CORRESPONDING member OF THE MAN WHO EATS IT. Assuredly, the sinew of the vein strengthens the Evil Inclination, which is its own kind, and therefore the children of Israel do not eat it. But the other nations may eat it, as they are of the side and kind of their angel Samael, for it strengthens their hearts.
—Zohar, Vayishlach 7:99-101

It is only the Zohar that makes this distinction. We do not see this explanation anywhere else—that eating of the sciatic nerve strengthens the hearts of the other nations.

One day, a non-Jew came to Rav Eliezer and asked him: "How is it that Jews are not permitted to eat this, that, and the sciatic nerve? We eat all of these things that the Bible does not permit Jews to eat, and we are stronger than the Jews, who are generally weak people. If you are closer to God, you should be stronger because someone who is a minister of the king certainly has more power than someone who is just outside the dominion of the king." Rav Eliezer answered that the Jewish people are like the heart, which is the center of the entire body. The heart is also the most delicate of all the bodily parts, and its blood must be pure. Therefore the Jew must also be pure.

The Zohar continues:

> Man has 248 members in his body, corresponding to the 248 positive Utterances in the Torah, and to the 248 angels, with whom the Shechinah is clothed, named after their Master. There are 365 sinews, corresponding to 365 prohibitory Precepts, and the sinew of the vein is one of them. They correspond to the 365 days of the year, that is, together with the ten days of penitence, the ninth of Av being one of them. It corresponds to the angel Samael, who is one of the 365 angels ruling over the 365 days of the year. The ninth of Av is one of the days of the year, and the sinew of the vein is one of the 365 sinews. Both belong to the same category. Thus, the Torah reads, "Therefore the children of Israel eat not of the sinew of the vein." The particle "et" (the) here includes the ninth of Av, when it is forbidden to eat and drink, being in the same category as the sinew of the vein.

> ...Rav Chiya says, "Had the strength of Jacob's thigh not weakened, Jacob would have prevailed, and Esau's power would have been broken Above and Below."
> —Zohar, Vayishlach 7:99-104

The Zohar explains that just as there are 365 nerves in the body, there are also 365 days in a year. There is one day a year to which Satan is connected—the 9th of Av; just as there is one nerve, the sciatic nerve, to which Satan is connected.

There are 248 members in the body—248, not 249, not 247, and there are 248 positive precepts, which are not rules that we must conform to or abide by, but are instead vehicles by which we can strengthen each and every energy-intelligence of these members of the body. That is why we recite the Kriat Shema, a very important prayer: "Hear, Israel, the Lord our God, the Lord is One." What makes this prayer so important? It is not because we must declare that the Lord is One—it has nothing to do with that. The Shema Israel is a device that provides me with 248 words, where each word connects with a particular part of the body.

When, through our negative activity, we have diminished the strength of our body parts and feel drained with no energy, we can recharge with the Kriat Shema. This is the reason for reading the Kriat Shema, which we also apply concentration with the meditation. Otherwise it is as though we have picked up the phone, tapped in the number but are not speaking. We are using something and not taking advantage of all that it offers. These 248 words constantly rejuvenate this internal essence of the 248 members.

There are 365 "do-not" precepts that connect to the 365 arteries and veins within the body. The 613 precepts are not about religion—there is no such thing as religion in Kabbalah. The 365 arteries and veins are the life system, the interaction between everything within the body. If we are unable to have an interaction where every part is assisting the other, then how can we have one unified whole? If everything is, by and of itself, a fragmented aspect of this one unified whole, how do we bring it all together?

We bring it together with Restriction, the Central Column, the balancing agent.

The many paths of spirituality, including Kabbalah, speak of love. Yet what are we meant to do if we simply do not like someone? It could be something from a prior incarnation that almost overwhelms us and coerces us into hating. As much as we understand and internalize the truths of spirituality, we are simply unable to love this particular individual. The Bible tells us not to hate, not to steal, not to murder—but the world continues to hate, to kill and to steal. The 365 "do-not" precepts require a meditation and a consciousness. If everything continues to be done by rote, we will have another 2,000 years of destruction and holocaust—and nothing is going to change. Rav Isaac Luria (the Ari), in his book Gate of Meditations, gives us a meditation for every single precept that can assist us in overcoming the problems we have to solve for getting rid of our desire to hate, steal, and so on. This meditation allows us to activate the internal energy of the precept.

We all have something that is not easy for us to overcome—and being told "not to" simply does not help. This is what Vayishlach is all about.

Beresheet 33:1 Jacob looked up and there was Esau, coming with his four hundred men; so he divided the children among Leah, Rachel, and the two maidservants. 2 He put the maidservants and their children in front, Leah and her children next, and Rachel and Joseph last.

The Order of Jacob's Wives

Jacob prepared himself to meet Esau, and he divided the nation that was with him—his family, the people of the world—into four parts. Jacob took his handmaids, Bilha and Zilpa—the two women with whom he had four children—and placed them in the first camp. Then he placed Leah and her children next, and at the rear he put Rachel and Joseph. There is nothing in the Zohar or the Writings of the Ari regarding this section. If we read it in a superficial manner, it is not flattering to Jacob. How could Jacob, a righteous man, an example we are meant to learn from, divide the camp in such a way? What would become of the children facing four hundred of Esau's wicked men? And why did he place Leah before Rachel? Can it be that he favored one wife over another? Does this mean that Jacob preferred Rachel over Leah? If so, then why is Jacob buried together with Leah in the Cave of Machpelah, while Rachel is buried alone on the way to Bethlehem?

Jacob reached a higher level of elevation when his name became "Israel," and Leah was on the level of Binah—meaning there was a greater degree of revealment of the Light of God. Rachel, on the other hand, was on the Malchut level. Therefore, Jacob wanted to expose Leah before he exposed Rachel. He felt that the Lightforce of the camp of Leah would be a greater deterrent than Rachel could have posed. But this then begs the question of why Jacob placed the handmaidens first—before Leah. The Zohar does not discuss this, and I have found no other mentions of why the arrangement should be so.

Making Peace

In general, this entire portion is cloaked in concealment; what is really taking place is found only on the inside. The reason Jacob organized the camp the way he did was not because he wanted to fight. It was because he wanted to make peace, and he did in fact succeed in doing so, for Esau arrived and nothing happened between them. There was no war. This is the power of Jacob, who attained a higher level of consciousness when his name was changed to Israel. Leah attained the level of Binah and Rachel Malchut in their respective revealing of the Light of the Creator. This is why Jacob wanted to expose Leah before Rachel.

In doing this, did Jacob not consider how he might appear? What would those of us who read the Bible many years later say of his action? It is very likely we might say that Jacob was wrong in his strategy.

What can be learned from Jacob here is that he was not concerned with what people might say because he knew he was with the Light. He knew what he was doing was right, even if the whole world was opposed to him—so he proceeded in peace. He was not afraid to make waves; he did not consider what people might say because for someone whose actions are about bringing about peace and goodness, there is nothing else to consider.

What we want to do at the Kabbalah Centres is similar to the actions of Jacob—to rid the world of its afflictions, and change the patterns that the world has endured for the last two thousand years.

All the troubles humankind has suffered can change if we arrange and configure things properly. If we abandon the old thought-patterns of humankind, everything will be different. This is what we are doing and why we are doing it all over the world. Of course there are those people who oppose the way we are working to make peace and bring goodness into the world. We are not afraid, though, and we will continue to make waves. We are not afraid of making waves. I prefer to proceed with confidence and make mistakes, than to know something is true but be too unsure to try it. The most important thing is to be connected with the Light, and this means that you must feel entirely certain that you are on the right path—that is, if all you want to do is to bring Light.

Jacob was not concerned about how he would appear. We do not have to be afraid when we make waves to change a chaotic situation. If each and every one of us makes waves in the right way, we not only can, but we will change the world.

3 He went on ahead and bowed down to the ground seven times as he approached his brother.

The Shechinah

Jacob bowed down seven times as he approached his brother, and Rav Elazar, in the Zohar, asks how Jacob—one of the greatest patriarchs, the one chosen to be the perfect portion of the Creator, and the one very close to Him—could bow down before the evil Esau, who stands on the side of another god? Is bowing down to Esau not the same as bowing down to another god or to the Other Side, as the evil one is also known? Esau is considered to be the very image of Satan, and Jacob bowed down to him. We have learned that one should not even say hello to a wicked person because it is a form of recognition, and, by doing so, we subject ourselves to that person's negativity.

The Zohar answers this question thus: "Who was bowing down to whom?" The Bible does not say that Jacob bowed down to Esau; it says that Jacob bowed until he reached his brother. Jacob was not bowing down to Esau; he bowed down to make a connection to God, to the Shechinah that made its appearance in front of him. The Shechinah walked ahead of Jacob, and ahead of the whole camp. And Jacob bowed down to indicate that he had never lost sight of what he was doing or why he was doing it.

Esau's Intent

Esau represents all that is negative, and Jacob represents what is good and pure—and yet they were brothers. Jacob was terrified and prayed because, although God had promised him that his descendants would be as numerous as the stars in the sky, he still felt death looming ahead of him.

Jacob said he had a gift of animals to appease his brother's anger. He sent his league of angels, clothed as soldiers, to face Esau. They said: "We are the people of Jacob." Esau saw the cattle and the angels who were there to protect Jacob. Jacob had his armaments, and in a moment he could have destroyed any foe. His message to Esau was: *Not only did I obtain Laban's goods, I also flourished in that place of negativity*, that place where Laban was greater in sorcery than any other person in history.

The significance of this story is that Esau wanted to kill his brother but he did not know how to do it. He moved forward to seize Jacob's neck to kill him, but instead he spared his life. Esau was trying to overcome all positivity. He did not intend for Jacob to walk away. Of course, these stories are all metaphors, allegories. The deeper meaning is that Jacob represents the Flawless Universe, and that Esau represents chaos. Scripture makes a point of stressing that this particular chapter relates to what would take place thousands of years later, at the time of the Redemption, when freedom from chaos could be achieved.

Today, chaos is still all-pervasive; there is no safe place on the planet. Terrorism persists all over the globe. There is nuclear waste in water. We cannot find fruits to eat that are free of radiation or that are not genetically modified. There are growing incidents of incurable diseases, and diseases thought to have been conquered for good have virulently returned. This portion is about what there *is* to do when everything around us seems to be crumbling—what there is to do when we feel no hope. Restriction is the solution. With the Lightforce of God we can simply switch on the Light, rather than expend our great efforts in other ways.

Holocausts and genocides throughout history were always perpetrated by people who felt that their mission was right—that it was even supported by God. Some of the greatest atrocities in human history were conducted "in the name of God," and both sides believed they were right, that God was on their side. The justification is always the same: It is always for the "right" reason. When looked at in this way, can we not see how the perpetrators of mass destruction and genocide are also victims in their own way?

Satan has infiltrated people's minds with his propaganda. This is the camouflage utilized by both sides. What is the one single formula for eliminating chaos? It is not readily acceptable to us because it is too simple. However, simple does not mean it is untrue. Everyone knows that when you turn on the Light, the darkness goes away.

There is no way out of chaos, and there are always justifications for chaos. How clever Satan is. He asks us, "Are you sure that if you turn the Light on, the darkness goes away?" How is Light brought into darkness? I personally do not know and I do not care how it happens. But I know it is true because I can see it. Though the eyes can deceive us, we all know that when a light is turned on, darkness disappears. Where does it go? Why does it come back? We need to know that the darkness will not return, unless a short circuit takes place.

There is only one form of Light that can effectively remove the darkness so that it will not come back—and this is Restriction, which is the purpose of this section. Why is it so difficult to be rid of diseases? Microbes perform brilliant maneuvers, outsmarting every known antibiotic. Diseases carried by bacteria persist because there is only one way to ultimately remove them—and that is by using the Lightforce of God to make them disappear, never to return. However, so often we create another short circuit, which brings chaos back into our lives. No one creates chaos for us; it

105

is we who actually go out and create chaos in our own lives. We may justify our actions but in the end, howsoever good the reasons are that give us permission to cause harm, we nevertheless create our own misery and illness because we have not done the proper restriction. Lack of restriction is the cause of a flawed and chaotic universe.

I have spent many years studying restriction, and finally I know why. This is an aspect of the Flawless Universe, and what I believe science means when it says one day the curtain will be removed, the underlying factors and principles will be seen for what they are. We cannot escape the fact that restriction is the only aspect of our lives that really exists. When we come to this realization—which we can only do through the study of Kabbalah—we will establish that the Lightforce of God is the only way we can eliminate chaos from our lives and our world. Jacob represents one simple thing: a consciousness of restriction.

Instinctively we are reactive people. What is our normal reaction to injury? To fight back. We feel justified in this. It is clear we did nothing wrong. This is not the case with Jacob, however. I am not saying that we should turn the other cheek; but striking back does not resolve the problem. Restrict instead; think first that you are not going to be reactive, then go back and strike the adversary. We need to exercise this consciousness. If it is just a question of a verbal dispute, one where we cannot agree with the other person's point of view and we become disturbed as a result—then, if we are disturbed, it means we are reactive. We need to become like Jacob and think how we can resolve the argument. It is not about being certain that we are right and then walking away. The argument will never end like that. Restrict on the level of Jacob, which is the balance of the Right and the Left—the Central Column. Jacob represents the power that is drawn down to us, and this is the only way.

4 But Esau ran to meet Jacob and embraced him; he fell upon his neck and kissed him, and they wept.

A Reunion Mixed with Love and Hate

Esau was on his way to kill Jacob. Jacob was fearful of this. Then all at once Esau ran towards him, hugged him, fell on his neck and kissed him, and then they both cried. What happened here? Rashi says that, as Esau saw his returning brother, Jacob, bowed down to him and extended compassion, then Esau hugged Jacob. Rashi is difficult to understand without the assistance of Kabbalah.

In the Torah Scroll, there are six dots above the Hebrew word *vayishakehu*, meaning "and he kissed him." It is unusual and always significant when there are dots above a word. Rashi states (in the name of Rav Shimon bar Yochai) that there is a spiritual law: Esau represents the other nations of the world, and he is obligated by Divine injunction to obey the law. The rule of God is that Esau must hate Jacob. But despite his passion to kill Jacob and his family at that moment, Esau does not do it. Rashi explains that this passion was transmuted into something else. The Bible is not referring to Esau as an individual, or to Jacob as an individual; nor is it speaking about the historical developments in a family saga. The Bible is concerned here with a development of the world—and this is far deeper. It relates to you and me because such an incident occurs each day of our lives.

Esau kissed his brother with such feeling, and yet only moments before his intention was evil. Esau felt and connected with the Light. This is what the six dots refer to. The dot is the smallest aspect of physicality. The moment Esau felt the pure level of the Lightforce of God, all enmity and hatred disappeared. Esau experienced the precept to hate but the moment he felt the Lightforce of God, this purest level of Light, everything of that nature disappeared from his heart.

When I was to visit Tunisia, the then Palestinian leader Yasser Arafat's headquarters, people asked me how I would dress. In over 23 years, no Jew had been seen there walking down the streets. My answer was that I intended to dress the way I always do. As I walked down the main street of Tunis, many, many Muslims asked to receive a blessing from me.

This is the only place here that a dot can be found on each letter. The power to be gained here from Jacob is that, even though Rashi and Rav Shimon say that Esau was commanded to hate Jacob, Esau nevertheless did Jacob no harm. When we distribute the Light properly, sending all the energy to the other nations, then they do not hate us. Hatred will only disappear when we reveal Light for the world—and for all the nations in it. Then the darkness disappears and all hatred vanishes. The power of these dots in this verse allows us to be determined to share the Light, and thereby prevent world problems and the hatred of Gentiles towards Jews. This truth cannot be repeated too often.

The Concealment of the Bible

The true meaning of this portion has remained in concealment, and it is our purpose now to reveal it—and not to do as many do, which is to speak about political positions and whether or not they agree with them. The six dots above the word *vayishakehu* should be particularly noted but they are not usually discussed. What can be said of this portion? That Jacob was prejudiced concerning his wives and handmaidens? Jacob was so stingy that he had to cross the river to fetch containers not even worth fifty cents? Or that Reuben slept with his father's wife, Bilhah? What insight can we get about the incident where Shimon and Levi circumcised the whole town; and the moment people were at their most vulnerable, Shimon and Levi slaughtered them all? The people we read about are meant to teach us; Jacob is meant to guide us. How can mainstream religion possibly make sense of this portion? Reuben, Shimon and Levi, like all the figures in the Bible, are there to show us how to behave properly; and yet, in this portion, we see how improperly they all behave. This is why there is not much discussion concerning this chapter.

What we are trying to do at the Kabbalah Centres is to allow people to understand what the Bible is really about. If an individual comes to read the Bible and he reads about a son who lies with his father's wife, a father who is frugal about fifty cents worth of old jars, and two men—Shimon and Levi—who kill people, it is understandable that this person will not want to hear any more. The concealment of the Bible is causing so much confusion. Those who truly wish to see what the Bible is have to take away the covering and see the truth that lies beneath—which is the wisdom of the Kabbalah.

Esau and the Law

The advantage of the six dots in this portion is that they are a direct connection to the Lightforce of God. The Lightforce cannot be touched. However, through these dots, we make the connection between the physical world and the immaterial Lightforce of God. Rashi quotes Rav Shimon who states that it is a law that Esau despises Jacob. Esau is considered to represent all the other nations of the world, except Islam. I do not know if everyone is aware of this law, which says that all the nations of the world hate Jews.

According to recent polls, fifty million people in the United States hate Jews. Of course not everyone in the United States is included in this poll. The Washington Post, which is considered to be a reasonably reliable newspaper, headlined: "America at War." This same article appeared in the New York Post as well. It was about two Jews in Afghanistan who got along with everyone except with each other—Isaac Weber and Isaac Levy, who were both from the western province. In the beginning, they thought they could help each other against the radical Islamist movement but it did not turn out that way. The biggest problem they had was that they were at war with each other, and spent time in jail because they each reported the other to the police, telling the Taliban lies, accusing each other of spying. Can you imagine two brothers doing this?

And, of course, there is the story of the two synagogues. I have told this for years and I only mean it as a joke, but it has a core of truth. The joke concerns a Jew who built a community because he wanted to live by himself, and the townspeople came to look the place over. The Jew showed them that he had an accountant's office, lawyer's office, and even a bakery, so that he would not lose touch with regular society. The visitors walked around the village and saw two synagogues, and they asked him why he needed two. Pointing to one of the buildings, he answered, "That's the one I don't go to." Now, however, this is not a joke anymore.

This is what I learned from my teacher, and what he learned from his teacher: The Jewish people have a united mission, and that mission is to provide the whole world with sustenance, which we do on Sukkot. All seventy nations of the world are fed by the work of the Jewish people, so that they can live in peace. I am not going into who is Jewish and who is not here; for me the Romans are Jewish. If you read history, you will see that one hundred thousand Jews were taken into slavery by Rome. What do you think happened to those Jews? Who do we think is Jewish in Italy? Why is this so significant now? Scripture shows us very clearly in this portion that it is a law that Esau hates Jacob.

Why are the Jews always the victims and the scapegoats? I have always said the greatest marketers are the Jews; they can make themselves the victim in any situation. Regarding this chapter, Rav Shimon affirms that Jews are always hated by Esau, who represents the other nations of the world. Why are we discussing this?

The Zohar and Rav Shimon say that Esau cried when he and his brother embraced, and when he kissed Jacob, he kissed him with all his heart. The gifts Jacob wanted to give Esau amounted to nothing in comparison to the Light embedded in Jacob that Esau felt and wanted for himself. Jacob fed his brother Light, and a non-Jew fed with Light will respond with love. I walked down the street in Tunis where Arafat lived, a place where people feared to come outside, even in the daytime. Yet many of the Muslims we passed there still asked me for a blessing. I have never had a problem with Muslims—only with the Jews. Those Jews who do not have the Light are filled with hatred, and thus they will in turn be hated. Esau wanted a blessing from Jacob, even though he intended to destroy him. Esau, the arch-enemy of Israel, someone who represents darkness and chaos, wept and asked Jacob for a blessing. This is what we can receive when listening to this reading on Shabbat.

We also receive blessings in the form of knowledge and understanding. Years ago, I had received from my teacher information about what this section dealt with, and this is the fact that medicine is pursuing the wrong path. Western medicine works to destroy disease with antibiotics, anti-cancer drugs and the like—the objective being to cut out the disease. Kabbalah says no! The disease is not the problem; disease is part of Creation, and it is necessary. Within every human being are cancer cells. So why does it strike some and not others?

The answer is that all of our consciousness should be directed towards Jacob, who is the Central Column. The information in this chapter is a spiritual tool, like the Third Meal of Shabbat. But remember that the most potent tool we can use is Restriction. Kabbalah Water has only one purpose: to strengthen the immune system. I have no doubts about anything the Zohar says. Not everyone has yet learned the seriousness of certainty.

Jacob made Esau kiss him with his energy. It is the destiny of the Jew to overcome this feeling of me rather than we, and so this is a very powerful section regarding how we can achieve connection with the Light.

5 Then Esau looked up and saw the women and children, and he said, "Who are these with you?" Jacob answered, "They are the children God has graciously given your servant." 6 Then the maidservants and their children approached and bowed down. 7 Next, Leah and her children came and bowed down. Last came Joseph and Rachel, and they bowed down. 8 Esau asked, "What do you mean by all these droves I met?" "To find favor in your eyes, my lord," he said. 9 But Esau said, "I already have plenty, my brother. Keep what you have for yourself." 10 "No, please!" said Jacob. "If I have found favor in your eyes, accept this offering from me. For to see your face is like seeing the face of God, now that you have received me favorably. 11 Please accept the blessing that I brought to you, for God has been gracious to me and I have all I need." And because Jacob insisted, Esau accepted it. 12 Then Esau said, "Let us be on our way; I'll accompany you." 13 But Jacob said to him, "My lord knows that the children are tender and that I must care for the ewes and cows that are nursing their young. If they are driven hard just one day, all the animals will die. 14 So let my lord go on ahead of his servant, while I move along slowly at the pace of the droves before me and that of the children, until I come to my lord in Seir." 15 Esau said, "Then let me leave some of my men with you." "But why do that?" Jacob asked. "Just let me find favor in the eyes of my lord."

16 So that day Esau started on his way back to Seir. 17 Jacob, however, went to Succoth, where he built a place for himself and made shelters for his livestock. That is why the place is called Succoth. 18 After Jacob came from Paddan Aram, he arrived safely at the city of Shechem in Canaan and camped within sight of the city. 19 For a hundred pieces of silver, he bought from the sons of Hamor, the father of Shechem, the plot of ground where he pitched his tent. 20 There he set up an altar and called it El Elohe Israel.

Beresheet 34:1 Now Dinah, the daughter of Leah had borne to Jacob, went out to visit the women of the land. 2 When Shechem, son of Hamor the Hivite, the ruler of that area, saw her, he took her, lay with her, and violated her. 3 His heart cleaved to Dinah, daughter of Jacob, and he loved the girl and spoke tenderly to her. 4 And Shechem said to his father Hamor, "Get me this girl as my wife." 5 When Jacob heard that his daughter Dinah had been defiled, his sons were in the fields with his livestock; so he kept quiet about it until they came home. 6 Then Shechem's father Hamor went out to talk with Jacob. 7 Now Jacob's sons had come in from the fields as soon as they heard what had happened. They were filled with grief and fury, because Shechem had done a disgraceful thing in Israel by lying with Jacob's daughter—a thing that should not be done. 8 But Hamor said to them, "My son Shechem has his heart set on your daughter. Please give her to him as his wife. 9 Intermarry with us; give us your daughters and take our daughters for yourselves. 10 You can settle among us; the land is open to you. Live in it, trade in it, and acquire property in it." 11 Then Shechem said to Dinah's father and brothers, "Let me find favor in your eyes, and I will give you whatever you ask. 12 Make the price for the bride and the gift I am to bring as great as you like, and I'll pay whatever you ask me. Only give me the girl as my wife." 13 Because their sister Dinah had been defiled, Jacob's sons replied deceitfully as they spoke to Shechem and his father Hamor. 14 They said to them, "We can't do such a thing; we can't give our sister to a man who is not circumcised. That would be a disgrace to us. 15 We will give our consent to you on one condition only: that you become like us by circumcising all your males. 16 Then we will give you our daughters and take your daughters for ourselves. We'll settle among you and become one people with you. 17 But if you will not agree to be circumcised, we'll take our sister and go." 18 Their proposal seemed good to Hamor and his son Shechem. 19 The young man, who was the most honored of his father's entire household, lost no time in doing what they said, because he was delighted with Jacob's daughter. 20 So Hamor and his son Shechem went to the gate of their city to speak to their fellow townsmen. 21 "These men are friendly toward us," they said. "Let them live in our land and trade in it; the land has plenty of room for them. We can marry their daughters and they can marry ours. 22 But the men will consent to live with us as one people only on the condition that our males are circumcised, as they themselves are. 23 Won't their livestock, their property and all their other animals become ours? So let us give our consent to them, and they will settle among us." 24 All the men who went out of the city gate agreed with Hamor and his son Shechem, and every male in the city was circumcised. 25 Three days later, while all of them were still in pain, two of Jacob's sons, Shimon and Levi, Dinah's brothers, took their swords and attacked the unsuspecting city, killing every male. 26 They put Hamor and his son Shechem to the sword and took Dinah from Shechem's house and left. 27 The sons of Jacob came upon the dead bodies and looted the city where their sister had been defiled. 28 They seized their flocks and herds and donkeys and everything else of theirs in the city and out in the fields. 29 They carried off all their wealth and all their women and children, taking as plunder everything in the houses. 30 Then Jacob said to Shimon and Levi, "You have brought trouble on me by making me a stench to the Canaanites and Perizzites, the people living in this land. We are few in number, and if they join forces against me and attack me, I and my household will be destroyed." 31 But

they replied, "Should he have treated our sister like a prostitute?"

Circumcision and the Light

Jacob had a daughter who was raped by Shechem, the son of Hamor the Hivite, and two of her brothers, Shimon and Levi, sought revenge. They murdered everyone in the city of the same name. The brothers first convinced the townspeople to be circumcised; and on the third day after the circumcision they killed every single one of them. These brothers were two chariots; they lived in two worlds at the same time—the Flawless Universe and the physical universe. How could these two people, who were connected to such a high level of consciousness, have deception and murder in their hearts? The Bible is meant to be the repository of law and order for civilization, not a blueprint for violent mayhem. How does any of this make sense without the Kabbalah?

We have to look to the Zohar to bring sense to this story. As a metaphor, the story has nothing to do with its literal meaning. Why is the Bible written in such a mysterious way? The story bears no resemblance to the true meaning of what the Bible wants to share with us. For example, the manner in which we hear about circumcision is teaching us that circumcision has turned into a ritual, when it is really supposed to be God's gift to humanity. If a circumcision is performed correctly, with the right meditations, it serves to convert negativity into positivity. But in the absence of any other answers, the Zohar will create an opening for the Light.

Beresheet 35:1 Then God said to Jacob, "Go up to Bethel and settle there, and build an altar there to God, who appeared to you when you were fleeing from your brother Esau." 2 So Jacob said to his household and to all who were with him, "Get rid of the foreign gods you have with you, and purify yourselves and change your clothes. 3 Then come, let us go up to Bethel, where I will build an altar to God, who answered me in the day of my distress and who has been with me wherever I have gone." 4 So they gave Jacob all the foreign gods they had and the rings in their ears, and Jacob buried them under the oak at Shechem. 5 Then they set out, and the terror of God fell upon the towns all around them so that no one pursued them. 6 Jacob and all the people with him came to Luz (that is, Bethel) in the land of Canaan. 7 There he built an altar, and he called the place El Bethel, because it was there that God revealed himself to him when he was fleeing from his brother. 8 Now Deborah, Rebecca's nurse, died and was buried under the oak below Bethel. So it was named Allon Bacuth. 9 After Jacob returned from Paddan Aram, God appeared to him again and blessed him. 10 God said to him, "Your name is Jacob, but you will no longer be called Jacob; your name will be Israel." So, he named him Israel.

Why Jacob is Still Called "Jacob" after Being Renamed "Israel"

The Zohar ponders instances where Jacob is called by his original name and not by the name "Israel," when it is written that he will no longer be called by the name "Jacob." A few verses later, it is "Jacob" who puts a memorial stone on the grave of Rachel—and he continues being called "Jacob" for the rest of the portion. In the beginning of the next portion, Vayeshev, the Zohar states that it is written "to be brave" where Elohim is written. This refers to judgment. And where the Tetragrammaton—*Yud*, *Hei*, *Vav*, and *Hei*—is written it refers to compassion. When the righteous are present in the world, the compassionate Name is used, and with it the Tetragrammaton energy is drawn into the world. When the wicked are present, *Elohim* energy appears.

11 And God said to him, "I am God Almighty; be fruitful and increase in number. A nation and a community of nations will come from you, and kings will come from your body. 12 The land I gave to Abraham and Isaac I also give to you, and I will give this land to your descendants after you." 13 Then God went up from him at the place where he had talked with him. 14 Jacob set up a stone pillar at the place where God had talked with him, and he poured out a drink offering on it; he also poured oil on it. 15 Jacob called the place where God had talked with him Bethel. 16 Then they moved on from Bethel. While they were still some distance from Ephrath, Rachel began to give birth and had a hard labor. 17 And as she was having great difficulty in childbirth, the midwife said to her, "Don't be afraid, for you have another son." 18 As her soul departed—for she was dying—she named her son Ben-Oni. But his father named him Benjamin. 19 So Rachel died and was buried on the way to Ephrath (that is, Bethlehem). 20 Over her tomb Jacob set up a pillar, and to this day that pillar marks Rachel's tomb. 21 Israel moved on again and pitched his tent beyond Migdal Eder. 22 While Israel was living in that region, Reuben went in and slept with his father's concubine Bilhah, and Israel heard of it. Jacob had twelve sons: 23 The sons of Leah: Reuben the firstborn of Jacob, Shimon, Levi, Judah, Issachar, and Zebulun. 24 The sons of Rachel: Joseph and Benjamin. 25 The

**sons of Rachel's maidservant Bilhah: Dan
and Naphtali. 26 The sons of Leah's maidservant Zilpah: Gad and Asher. These were
the sons of Jacob, who were born to him in
Paddan Aram. 27 Jacob came home to his father Isaac in Mamre, near Kiriath Arba (that
is, Hebron), where Abraham and Isaac had
lived. 28 Isaac lived a hundred and eighty
years. 29 Then he breathed his last and died
and was gathered to his people, old and
full of years. And his sons Esau and Jacob
buried him.**

Jacob and Israel

The Zohar says:

> As Rav Elazar and Rav Yosi were walking together, Rav Yosi
> said, "What you said is true, that Jacob is the most perfect
> of the fathers. He includes all sides, NAMELY RIGHT
> AND LEFT. For that reason, he was called Israel, as it is
> written, "Your name shall not be called any more Jacob, but
> Israel shall be your name, and He called his name Israel."
> (Beresheet 35:10) Why then, HE INSISTED, does the
> Holy One, blessed be He, repeatedly call him Jacob as he
> was commonly called before? What then is the meaning of,
> "your name shall not be called any more Jacob?"
>
> He replies, "You have spoken well. THIS IS A GOOD
> QUESTION." He then quoted the verse, "The Lord shall
> go forth as a mighty man, He shall stir up ardor like a man
> of war," (Yeshayah 42:13) which has already been explained.
> Yet come and behold, it is written, "as a mighty man" instead

of "a mighty man," and "like a man of war" instead of "a man of war."

HE EXPLAINS, We learned that the Lord refers uniformly to Mercy, and the Name of the Holy One, blessed be He, is *Yud, Hei, Vav*, and *Hei*, as it is written, "I am the Lord (*Yud, Hei, Vav*, and *Hei*): that is My Name." (Yeshayah 42:8) Yet we see that He is sometimes called Elohim, which everywhere alludes to Judgment. Whenever there are many righteous in the world, His Name is *Yud, Hei, Vav*, and *Hei*, and He is called Mercy. But when the wicked multiply in the world, His Name is *Elohim*, and He is thus called. When Jacob is not among his enemies or in a foreign country, he is called Israel, but when he is among foes or out of Israel, he is called Jacob.
—Zohar, Vayishlach 16:167-169

The question is not yet answered, however, because it is written that "Jacob settled," when Jacob was in the land of Israel. There is a difference between the names "Jacob" and "Israel." When we are addressing the head, we are addressing "Israel," and when Israel is without a head it is call "Jacob."

He replies, "I said, in the beginning, that just as the Holy One, blessed be He, is sometimes called *Yud, Hei, Vav*, and *Hei* and sometimes *Elohim*, ACCORDING TO THE GRADE, so Jacob is sometimes called Israel and sometimes Jacob, all according to certain grades. And the words, 'shall not be called any more Jacob,' MEAN THAT he will not have this name only, JACOB, BUT TWO NAMES, JACOB AND ISRAEL, ACCORDING TO HIS GRADE."
—Zohar, Vayishlach 16:171

Rav Eliezer answers that the alternating names are because "Israel" is attached to the Upper Triangle and "Jacob" is attached to the Lower Triangle.

The Zohar continues:

He said, "So it was with Abraham, about whom it is written, 'Neither shall your name any more be called Abram, but your name shall be Abraham.' (Beresheet 17:5) YET THIS DOES NOT MEAN THAT HE WILL BE CALLED BY TWO NAMES, ABRAM AND ABRAHAM, BUT RATHER ONLY ABRAHAM." He answers, "The scripture says, 'but YOUR NAME SHALL BE (HEB. *VEHAYAH*) ABRAHAM,' therefore only this name remained. Yet here the word *vehayah* is not used. Rather, it reads, 'but Israel shall be (Heb. *yih'yeh*) your name.' It does not read, 'Israel shall be (Heb. *vehayah*) your name,' and ACCORDING TO THIS, it is sufficient to call him Israel on only one occasion, TO FULFILL THE VERSE, WHICH READS, 'BUT ISRAEL SHALL BE YOUR NAME.' This is all the more true because although he is sometimes called Jacob, there are other times he is called Israel. When his sons are adorned with priests and Levites, he will be called by the name ISRAEL for all times."
—Zohar, Vayishlach 16:172

Jacob operated on two levels, whereas Abraham operated on only one level.

Beresheet 36:1 These are the generations of
Esau, who is Edom. 2 Esau took his wives
from the women of Canaan: Adah, daughter
of Elon the Hittite, and Oholibamah, daughter of Anah and granddaughter of Zibeon
the Hivite, 3 also Basemath, daughter of
Ishmael and sister of Nebaioth. 4 Adah bore
Eliphaz to Esau, Basemath bore Reuel, 5 and
Oholibamah bore Jeush, Jalam, and Korah.
These were the sons of Esau, who were born
to him in Canaan. 6 Esau took his wives and
sons and daughters and all the souls of his
household, as well as his livestock and all his
other animals and all the goods he had ac-
quired in Canaan, and moved to a land some
distance from his brother Jacob. 7 Their possessions were too great for them to remain
together; the land where they were staying
could not support them both because of their
livestock. 8 So Esau, who is Edom, settled in
the hill country of Seir. 9 These are the generations of Esau, the father of the Edomites in
the hill country of Seir. 10 These are the names
of Esau's sons: Eliphaz, the son of Esau's
wife Adah, and Reuel, the son of Esau's wife
Basemath. 11 The sons of Eliphaz: Teman,
Omar, Zepho, Gatam, and Kenaz. 12 Esau's
son Eliphaz also had a concubine named
Timna, who bore him Amalek. These were
grandsons of Esau's wife Adah. 13 The sons
of Reuel: Nahath, Zerah, Shammah, and
Mizzah. These were the grandsons of Esau's
wife Basemath. 14 The sons of Esau's wife
Oholibamah, daughter of Anah and grand-

daughter of Zibeon, whom she bore to Esau: Jeush, Jalam, and Korah. 15 These were the chiefs among Esau's descendants: The sons of Eliphaz, the firstborn of Esau: Chiefs Teman, Omar, Zepho, Kenaz, 16 Korah, Gatam, and Amalek. These were the chiefs descended from Eliphaz in Edom; they were grandsons of Adah. 17 The sons of Esau's son Reuel: Chiefs Nahath, Zerah, Shammah, and Mizzah. These were the chiefs descended from Reuel in Edom; they were grandsons of Esau's wife Basemath. 18 The sons of Esau's wife Oholibamah: Chiefs Jeush, Jalam, and Korah. These were the chiefs descended from Esau's wife Oholibamah, daughter of Anah. 19 These were the sons of Esau, who is Edom, and these were their chiefs. 20 These were the sons of Seir the Horite, who were living in the region: Lotan, Shobal, Zibeon, Anah, 21 Dishon, Ezer, and Dishan. These sons of Seir in Edom were Horite chiefs. 22 The sons of Lotan: Hori and Homam. Timna was Lotan's sister. 23 The sons of Shobal: Alvan, Manahath, Ebal, Shepho, and Onam. 24 The sons of Zibeon: Aiah and Anah. This is the Anah who discovered the hot springs in the desert while he was grazing the donkeys of his father Zibeon. 25 The children of Anah: Dishon and Oholibamah, daughter of Anah. 26 The sons of Dishon: Hemdan, Eshban, Ithran, and Keran. 27 The sons of Ezer: Bilhan, Zaavan, and Akan. 28 The sons of Dishan: Uz and Aran. 29 These were the Horite chiefs: Lotan, Shobal, Zibeon, Anah,

30 Dishon, Ezer, and Dishan. These were the Horite chiefs, according to their divisions, in the land of Seir. 31 These were the kings who reigned in Edom before any Israelite king reigned: 32 Bela, son of Beor, became king of Edom. His city was named Dinhabah. 33 When Bela died, Jobab, son of Zerah from Bozrah, succeeded him as king. 34 When Jobab died, Husham from the land of the Temanites succeeded him as king. 35 When Husham died, Hadad, son of Bedad, who defeated Midian in the country of Moab, succeeded him as king. His city was named Avith. 36 When Hadad died, Samlah from Masrekah succeeded him as king. 37 When Samlah died, Shaul from Rehoboth on the river succeeded him as king. 38 When Shaul died, Baal-Hanan, son of Acbor, succeeded him as king. 39 When Baal-Hanan, son of Acbor, died, Hadad succeeded him as king. His city was named Pau, and his wife's name was Mehetabel, daughter of Matred, the daughter of Me-Zahab. 40 These were the chiefs descended from Esau, by name, according to their clans and regions: Timna, Alvah, Jetheth, 41 Oholibamah, Elah, Pinon, 42 Kenaz, Teman, Mibzar, 43 Magdiel, and Iram. These were the chiefs of Edom, according to their settlements in the land they occupied. This was Esau, the father of the Edomites.

BOOK OF BERESHEET:

Portion of Vayeshev

PORTION OF VAYESHEV

Beresheet 37:1 And Jacob dwelt in the land where his father had stayed, the land of Canaan.

Spiritual Work and Certainty

In the portion of Vayeshev, the commentators discuss the words "And Jacob dwelt…," the implication here being that Jacob settled down and lived complacently. However, just because the Bible says "Jacob dwelt" does not mean that he was idle, as is often suggested by some commentators.

It appears that Jacob wanted a little peace and quiet after all the trials and tribulations he had been through. In the past, as we have seen, Esau wanted to kill him; then Esau's son, Eliphaz, came to kill him but instead took all his money; Laban took advantage of Jacob and made him work for fourteen years in return for Laban's daughters; and next, when he arrived in Israel, his daughter, Dinah, was raped by Shechem, son of Hamor; and finally, as soon as Jacob wanted peace and quiet, the incident with Joseph occurred. All of these incidents instruct us that, in this world, it is impossible to rest for even a minute. Even those who have worked hard, as Jacob did, still have more left to do.

The purpose of all spiritual work is to become attached to the Tree of Life, and thereby to emerge from chaos. There must be a certainty that things will work out at the end of the process though, even if there are ups and downs at the present moment. It is simply not possible to equivocate about this.

Looking for Comfort

Vayeshev encompasses all that has taken place in the narrative before now. The word *vayehsev* means "he sat," and the Zohar and all commentators explain that this singular word tells much. Jacob worked for years in exile for Laban, a father-in-law who made bitter every moment of his life. Jacob withstood evil sorcery and witchcraft during the twenty-two years he was in Laban's employ but that was also the time and place he met his wives. Jacob returned to his homeland, to Canaan, when his work was done, understandably looking forward to a period of contented retirement.

What the story reveals is that if we seek comfort, we should look for the reverse; it is only then that we can achieve the things in life that we all truly cherish. This is the basic instruction expressed in the old adage: "There is no rest for the weary." The Bible teaches us similarly by showing that, when we seek retirement, we can expect the worst instead. We can expect to enter another level of existence. However, a life without problems will not be accompanied by the idea that we have no more contributions to make in this world. When we have had a hard day and hope to relax, this is the moment when the telephone rings and everything suddenly needs our attention. I certainly hope, though, that none of us ever has to experience anything like the sale of Joseph by his brothers.

2 These are the generations of Jacob. Joseph, a young man of seventeen, was tending the flocks with his brothers, the sons of Bilhah and the sons of Zilpah, his father's wives, and he brought their father a bad report about them.

Those Who Help Us Connect and the Slander of Jacob

This verse begins with the grand statement: "These are the generations of Jacob," and then it says "Joseph." What does this mean? Jacob has other children, so why does the Bible mention only Joseph? And in the same verse it is written that Joseph slandered his brothers to their father. How is this to be understood? The Zohar says that Joseph symbolizes the Central Column, and that "These are the generations of Jacob. Joseph..." is not stating that Joseph is the most beloved son, rather it indicates that Jacob is symbolized by the Central Column of Tiferet in the Upper Triangle of the Magen David (Shield of David), and that Joseph is the Central Column of the Lower Triangle in Yesod.

In the Zohar it says that this simple story in the Bible is only a preparation for entering into the gate of its true inner meaning. Rav Shimon bar Yochai states that the Bible on its own is a code that has no literal meaning. Whenever we introduce commentators here, we do so as an aid for us to enter and delve into the Bible's inner meaning. Since this portion is one of the most confused narratives in the whole Torah, we must realize that an opportunity is being presented; for, where there is confusion and mystery, there is also the inner force of the Light available to us whenever we seek to understand and investigate.

With this in mind, we can begin to comprehend that Joseph is not yet a *tzadik*, not yet a righteous man. He becomes a *tzadik* later in the story—after he refuses the advances of Potiphar's wife, who attempted to seduce him. At this point in the story, as one of the twelve sons of Jacob, he was one of the twelve Chariots. Joseph is known as the Chariot of Yesod—the one who connects this world to the world of the Tree of Life. We engage the assistance of these chariots, not because of their unusual inclination or choice, but because of their desire to connect the world of the Tree of Knowledge of Good and Evil (the world we live in, the World of Illusion) to the Tree of Life. As a result of their desire, they have attained a level of communication with the higher realms. They are connected and they assist us to connect to the Tree of Life.

Rashi says that when Joseph spoke ill of his brothers to his father, this was considered slander. There were three slanderous things he said. The first was that they were eating the living meat of animals, amputating them limb by limb—and this is a sin. Not to eat "a live limb" is one of the Seven Commandments of the children of Noah. No one is allowed to take an animal and cut it up while it is still alive. As if the slander were not enough in itself, it is even more disturbing to find that it was not even true. The second accusation, as Rashi tells us, is that Joseph told Jacob that the sons of Bilhah (who was a surrogate mother to him) were being treated like slaves by the sons of Leah—and this was also untrue. The third slanderous statement made by Joseph was that his brothers were doing sexually perverse, unnatural things, which was also not true.

Who can believe that Joseph could say things like this? We are speaking about Joseph the Righteous here. Would these slanders have pleased his father? Rashi says that, because Joseph maligned his brothers, he had to pay a price. Later on in the story, the brothers sold Joseph as a slave—an action that was then punishable by death. These brothers, of whom we are speaking, are also Chariots, making this one of the most exceptionally difficult chapters in the whole Bible.

According to the teachings of Rav Shimon bar Yochai, the consequence of the "live limb" tale was that the brothers dipped Joseph's garment in the blood of an animal they had slaughtered, and then brought it to their father. This was how the punishment came to fit the crime: an animal on account of an animal. Regarding the second accusation, Joseph was sold into slavery on account of his slurs claiming that the sons of Bilhah were treated like slaves. Joseph paid for this second accusation with imprisonment. His third slanderous statement—that his brothers performed perverse sexual acts—was met with the counter-accusation that he forced himself on the wife of Potiphar.

Rashi says that every action has a matching response. Therefore, the three things that Joseph told his father were technically not slander. Rashi explains that when scripture refers to the talk between Joseph and his father Jacob, it tells us that they were discussing the laws of the universe and the three aspects of negative activity. They discussed the negative activity of idol worship, which is when an individual relates to another as if they are a god and the supplicant, a slave. They discussed sexual deviations, as well as the issue of eating the "live limb;" and this is because slander is analogous to sucking someone's blood without killing them. The Bible wants to teach us that each of these behaviors covers all categories, and that for each, there is a matching response or consequence.

The lesson here is that if we do something negative, there is a price to pay—and this is an inviolable cosmic law. The Bible is also telling us that the way to undo the cosmic imprint made yesterday is to connect to the Central Column, the force of Resistance.

Through the portion of Vayeshev we are connecting to the force of energy that can terminate negative records or imprints. The Zohar says that we have to suffer the experience, the discomfort, and the pain that are our due. But if we are connected to Joseph, and if we begin to understand that the force of Resistance or Restriction has to become part of our lives, this knowledge will make the load lighter to bear and in the end, we will realize that what we experience has been for our own good.

Through this portion we gain a great deal from Joseph. This seemingly ridiculous chapter exists to focus us on the real meaning of its story—which is that it is the force of Resistance we can use to erase any negative recording.

The Zohar relates the following story:

> Rav Chiya and Rav Yosi were walking along the way and chanced upon a mountain. They found two men walking, and at the same time a man coming, who said to them: "Please, I pray you, give me a piece of bread, for I have been lost in the desert for two days and have had nothing to eat." One of the men went aside, took out the provision he brought with him for the way and gave it to him; he fed him and gave him drink. His companion said to him, "What shall you do when you need food? For as for me, I will eat my own AND SHALL GIVE YOU NOTHING." He said to him, "I do not rely upon YOUR FOOD." The poor man sat by him until he had eaten all he had, and he gave the remaining bread to the poor man for the road. And he went away.
>
> Rav Chiya said, "The Holy One, blessed be He, did not wish it to be done by us." Rav Yosi said, "Perhaps there is an impending sentence upon that man, and the Holy

One, blessed be He, wanted to put this in his way in order to save him." While they were walking the man became exhausted DUE TO HUNGER. His companion said to him, "Did I not tell you not to give your bread to another?" Rav Chiya said to Rav Yosi, "We have food with us, let us give him some to eat." Rav Yosi said, "Do you wish to take away his merit? Let us go and see, for surely death follows in his footsteps." MEANING THAT THE DANGER OF DEATH IS FOLLOWING HIM and the Holy One, blessed be He, wishes to prepare a merit for him in order to save him.

Meanwhile, the man sat to sleep under a tree. His friend went further and sat in a different place. Rav Yosi said to Rav Chiya, "Let us sit down and watch, for surely the Holy One, blessed be He, intends to perform a miracle by him." They stood up and waited. While they were waiting, they saw a fiery rattlesnake standing by him. Rav Chiya said. "Woe unto that man, for he is about to die." Rav Yosi said, "This man is worthy of a miracle of the Holy One, blessed be He." A snake then came down the tree with the intention of killing him. The rattlesnake attacked the snake and killed it. Then the rattlesnake turned his head and went on his way.
—Zohar, Behar 9:58-60

The first snake that came to bite the man as he slept was his destiny. It was inevitable that this incident had to occur but the man saved his own life by the action of giving away his food. If we have difficulties, problems, pain, and suffering, for there to be a happy ending what is required is the power of Resistance that is necessary to get through the chaos. Joseph had to be sold into slavery but was he truly a slave? No. Shortly thereafter, he became the viceroy of Potiphar. Joseph rose above it all. All this is given to us in Vayeshev so that each time this reading is heard, we can tap into the energy of the Central Column and raise our consciousness. This great opportunity is something not to be wasted.

3 Now Israel loved Joseph more than any of his other sons, because he had been born to him in his old age; and he made a striped robe of many colors for him. 4 When his brothers saw that their father loved him more than any of them, they hated him and could not speak a kind word to him. 5 Joseph dreamt a dream, and when he told it to his brothers, they hated him all the more. 6 He said to them, "Listen to this dream I had: 7 We were binding sheaves of grain out in the field when suddenly my sheaf rose and stood upright, while your sheaves gathered around mine and bowed down to it." 8 His brothers said to him, "Do you intend to reign over us? Will you actually rule us?" And they hated him all the more because of his dream and what he had said. 9 Then he had another dream, and he told it to his brothers. "Listen," he said, "I had another dream, and this time the sun and moon and eleven stars were bowing down to me."

Preference of One Child Over Another

The portion of Vayeshev is one of the few that contains so much contradiction, and is so mind-boggling that without the Zohar, I do not know how we could ever maintain faith in the Bible.

This section speaks of Jacob's preference for Joseph over his other sons. While it is true that parents can have a preference for one child over another, the wise parent realizes it is in the children's best interest to conceal that feeling of preference and to display love equally to all their children. Jacob seems not to abide by this rule. Why? The scripture says that Jacob loved Joseph more because Joseph was born when Jacob was old. However, Joseph had a younger brother Benjamin so why did Jacob not display that unconditional love to Benjamin as well? Joseph was born from his most beloved wife, Rachel—but then so was Benjamin.

Love and Energetic Similarity

The love described between Jacob and Joseph is not an ordinary love. If the Bible were talking about ordinary love, then the entire story in this portion would be ridiculous. How could a man like Jacob love only one child and not the rest of his children? What this section is discussing is how love balances forms. Let me explain.

Jacob indicates Tiferet, the Central Column of the Upper Triangle in the Shield of David; whereas Joseph indicates Yesod, the Central Column of the Lower Triangle. Both are a median, signifying balance—and this is what Jacob or Israel, as he was soon called, loved about Joseph. This story is all about the balance of form.

Israel loved Joseph because Joseph supplied the force of the Central Column, which is useful to us now. When we listen to this reading, we make contact with the framework of Yesod, through Joseph the Righteous. Joseph and Jacob were identical in spiritual form, in that, on a metaphysical level, the Light of Tiferet travels to Yesod and thus transfers the Light from Jacob to Joseph.

When the Vayeshev narrative talks about fraternal hatred, we must remember that what is being referred to here are the twelve tribes—people who are vehicles or Chariots for forces of energy. Matters of love and hate, so familiar to us these days, are not what is being spoken about here. The hatred of the brothers was not an ordinary hatred. The brothers were on a different spiritual level from Joseph, meaning they were not balanced in form. The loathing they felt towards Joseph was so strong that they would not even greet him in passing, and this was due to the disconnection between their different levels.

Chariots and their Relationship with the Physical World and the Tree of Life Reality

Jacob is one of the seven Chariots of the Sefirot of the Tree of Life. Why are certain people of the Bible invited into the Sukkah? Kabbalah explains that they are invited because they are a symbol of the seven energies in our universe. Jacob represents one of these seven Chariots (Tiferet), and through him we strive to divorce ourselves from the chaos around us.

How can we extract ourselves from chaos? How can we live in the midst of this environment of discord and yet, simultaneously maintain a connection with the Flawless Universe? How can we exist in the physical universe, and at the same time taste the Tree of Life consciousness? This, however, is what a chariot does. Jacob's other sons were also Chariots. This story describes people at a much higher spiritual level than most of us—yet it still says that the brothers hated Joseph.

The brothers would bring rumors to their father, speaking evil tongue (lashon hara). Jacob was well aware of the friction in his family. Yet despite this he made for Joseph a special coat, thereby arousing the perception in the brothers that their father loved Joseph more—thus making him hated more than ever. Then Joseph related some of his dreams to them, which provoked them still further: "What do you mean you are going to be our ruler," they asked. The brothers were so jealous of Joseph that Jacob asked Joseph why he told his brothers about the dreams.

It is hard to understand how these *tzadikim* (righteous people) were so filled with hatred. The Zohar and the Talmud explain that this hatred persisted and was firmly established among all of the people. It is what eventually caused the destruction of the Holy Temple in Jerusalem. Why is jealousy the cause of such intense hatred, and why does it cause such misery? It is human nature to want what others have, and even to ask: "Why don't I have?" But does our desire involve depriving others so that we can have what they have? The reason jealousy has such an extraordinary capacity for evil is because of how it functions. When a thief steals, at least he or she benefits, since something at least was obtained by someone. Whether they are ultimately punished for the theft is another discussion.

However, in the case of jealousy or evil eye (Heb. *ayin hara*), an individual who feels jealous not only feels a lack because they see and want what they do not have, they also resent someone else for having it—and this inserts negative energy into the person whom they envy. The jealous person not only creates a problem for the object of their envy but for all of the trouble elicited by the evil eye—and what did they receive for this? They did not even come into possession of what they were missing. Jealousy of others gains nothing but hatred.

The Zohar explains that when chaos reigns in a family it is because of the existence of jealousy and envy. Both character flaws inflict an enormous measure of chaos. When we experience negative emotions about someone who might actually have done us wrong, we validate our hatred and envy. We may ask why we should turn the other cheek. If one is truly intent on removing chaos, it is not wise to dwell on how someone has something that we do not have. It is a paradox—the same paradox that we have here in this Bible portion. Jacob gave his son, Joseph, a coat, knowing full well that his other sons already hated Joseph. The giving of the coat is a metaphor. Jacob was not creating more reasons for hatred. Instead, he was demonstrating what takes place in this physical dimension of ours. Only the absence of envy—which is unity—will save us. This is one of the reasons we embrace each other as we do in the Kabbalah Centres, and it is the reason for the various prayers we perform—it is not to be different. Kabbalah is the only path we can take to remove the chaos from our lives, chaos that stretches from the very beginning to the present time.

There is an old saying: "He would sell his own mother down the river." People with that kind of selfish nature draw down upon themselves their own hardships. Why? When we hate or are envious, all we do is compound chaos. This portion is a singular opportunity to reach a dimension where we can manifest the understanding that even our worst enemy must always be treated with human dignity. And in this way we will be able to remove chaos. It must be understood that everyone, even our enemies, has a spark of God in them. We cannot think, "No, he is full of Satan!" I am not here to suggest that we extend mercy to tyrants, though. Politics and spirituality do not necessarily mix. On this level each person must decide for themselves. There is no law about how to direct our consciousness. Let us confine our ideas to our own lives, where we individually choose not to participate in such an evil. I do not want to be a judge but we are all guilty of being judgmental. Our minds justify the hatred we extend to people. This is what we learn from reading this section.

Why did Joseph decide to tell his brothers about his dream, which clearly suggested he was better than them? Why did Jacob choose to give Joseph the coat of many colors, which would arouse jealousy in the hearts of the brothers? Could he not have been more discreet?

Jacob and Joseph, who were vehicles or Chariots for the Central Column, want to teach us about true concern. They show that, when we act with responsibility and concern, we may see the entire quantum. The minute we decide that we are with the Light, we can no longer allow ourselves to behave the way we have previously acted. Concern does not mean only taking responsibility and caring for our own things, such as the trifle of whether a shirt is dirty or wrinkled. Concern is for what is outside of ourselves.

For example, when parents refuse to be concerned about their surroundings by improving and advancing all the time, this will impose upon their children the responsibility of amending the deeds of these parents. Therefore, we must guide our children from an early age by being an example, by teaching them in turn to be concerned and responsible. We cannot be concerned now and again; true concern is to be alert at all times.

The Coat Jacob Gave to Joseph

The first letters of the Hebrew verse, וְעָשָׂה לוֹ כְּתֹנֶת, meaning "he made him a striped coat"—*Vav, Lamed, Kaf*—are equivalent to the word קוֹל, which means "voice." According to the Zohar, "voice" is Zeir Anpin, the "Small Face" of the Tree of Life. This teaches us that Jacob did not give Joseph a material garment but a formula for connecting to the Tree of Life, to a world without chaos.

Jacob gave Joseph "the coat" knowing it would bring suffering. He was aware of the hatred and chaos the coat would elicit. But he also knew that Joseph would need it for his work, and that it was for the greater good. He understood that there is another universe, an immaterial one, and that, while we are in this physical world, Satan is the ruler. Make no mistake about it, there is a parallel universe, and with the study of Kabbalah we learn how we can connect to the

Flawless Universe and leave this darkened realm, with all of its hate and chaos, behind. This portion gives us the strength to deal with our chaos and take responsibility without excuses or complaints.

The Nature of Dreams, and Joseph's Separation

A dream is similar to prophecy, but it can be half false and half true. It is not worthwhile to recount a dream, except to someone who loves you. Because of his brothers' "hatred," the resolution of Joseph's dream was deferred until much later. On the other hand, the prisoners who told Joseph their dreams received the right interpretations immediately.

Our actions create the recording of a dream. Through the dreams, Joseph's brothers understood that Joseph was removed from the framework of the kingdom of the twelve tribes. What was transpiring was indeed separation, and not hatred. When the Bible uses the word "hated" it refers to a change of level. This is similar to when Jacob was connected to Rachel; he was on a different level then than he was when he became Israel and was connected to Leah. Jealousy is mentioned to indicate their understanding that the messages they received are on different levels, on different planes—as it is in a dream. This tells us something about dreams and, if we are meritorious, it also tells us something about the future.

10 When he told his father as well as his brothers, his father rebuked him and said, "What is this dream you had? Will your mother and I and your brothers actually come and bow down to the ground before you?" 11 His brothers were jealous of him, but his father kept the matter in mind.

Jacob Kept the Matter in Mind

What is the meaning of the verse that says Jacob "kept the matter in mind."? What was Jacob keeping in mind? Although the Bible states that Jacob rebuked Joseph, we know, however, that this is referring to a world that is on a different level of consciousness. Jacob saw the future development of events, and that this was all a part of the program of redemption. Jacob saw the causes and the effects, which happens when a person is connected to the Light. This is what we connect to here in this portion.

In the very next verse, it is written that his brothers went to herd the sheep in Shechem. Therefore, "and his father kept the matter in mind" is telling us that he, Jacob, had a vision that they were going to Shechem. Jacob (who had become "Israel" at this stage) saw, from his elevated consciousness, the purpose of Shechem.

12 Now his brothers had gone to graze their father's flocks near Shechem.

Dots Above the Word Et and the Greatness of Smallness

There are no vowels or cantillation notes in the Torah Scroll; yet in this verse, above the Hebrew word *et*, the smallest word in the language, there are two dots. Dots above a word in the Torah Scroll indicate that there is an emphasis on that word. The word *et* is made up of the first and the last letter of the Hebrew alphabet— א *Alef* and ת *Tav*—indicating that the word *et* encompasses all, and represents the whole world. This universe was created by means of the Hebrew letters, all of which are the seeds of Creation.

What is a dot, and why is a dot used to emphasize a word? A dot is the smallest thing anyone can see. In the spiritual realm, what is less is more, and what is more is less. We are now in an era of spirituality, where the small is more important than the great.

The word *et*, in fact, has no meaning and, therefore, it has no limitations. It is what kabbalists have described as the most important word. Just as this word *et*, which has no meaning, embraces everything from the *Alef* to the *Tav*, the two dots above the word *et* are an added opportunity to tap into the Lightforce of the Tree of Life. Because it has the smallest degree of physicality, it is able to act as a vessel of great Light.

This is a tenet of contemporary science too. Where there is the least physicality, there is the greatest amount of energy. Consider the size of old-fashioned telephone cables, and their severe limitations. Now we have fiber-optics, where half a million phone calls can be put through a single cable at one time. In the physical reality, what is more is always less. So we are given the opportunity with this reading to tap into the realm of the Tree of Life.

The Shechinah Was with the Brothers

The Hebrew word *et*, with one dot above each letter, is found in the verse, "his brothers had gone to tend their father's sheep in Shechem" (present day Nablus). There are only ten times in the entire Torah Scroll where dots appear above the Hebrew letters, and the dots above the word *et* is one such occasion. The word *et* functions in Hebrew as a transitive preposition. The Zohar notes that this word is superfluous since, even without the word *et* the verse would be clear. There is no translation for the word *et* in English or in any other language. It is always unnecessary, and therefore there must always be some secret meaning to each and every *et*, especially in this case. The reason *et* is written here is to include the Shechinah (the Divine Presence) with them. Therefore, we know that the Creator was present when they went to Shechem and thought of selling Joseph.

This leaves us with many questions. What does it matter if the Shechinah was with them? We do not find dots in the Torah Scroll every time the Shechinah is with someone, so why does it call for two dots in this case? This is the only instance where there are dots when the Shechinah is present with someone. When we read that Abraham was in the presence of the Shechinah, there are no dots. How are we to understand that the Creator was involved with the selling of Joseph to the Egyptians? The Ten Holy Martyrs, who were executed by the Romans during the time of the destruction of the Second Temple, are said to have been the reincarnation of Joseph's brothers. They were killed on account of the sin of selling Joseph in their past incarnation. If they were meant to sell him, why then were they punished? This is all very difficult to understand.

The Midrash, the Talmud, and the Zohar explain it to us very clearly. The trip the brothers took to Shechem, which resulted in the sale of Joseph and his ascent to become the viceroy of Egypt, was made for the sake of their provisions of food and their welfare during the coming years of famine. As Joseph himself said, "It was for sustenance that the Lord sent me here before you." The descent into Egypt was, however, also to be a necessity for all future generations, and for the giving of the Torah. Without the cleansing of Egypt, we would not have been prepared to receive the Torah.

It is clear that it was Joseph's destiny to go to Egypt. But, at the same time, this does not mean that his brothers were obliged to sell him. Since it was necessary for Joseph to go down to Egypt, the Creator could have arranged another way for him to get there. His arrival in Egypt was vital, not only for his own personal completion but also for that of the entire world. All that transpired happened to instruct us.

13 And Israel said to Joseph, "As you know, your brothers are grazing the flocks near Shechem. Come, and I will send you to them." "Here I am," he replied. 14 So he said to him, "Go and see if all is well with your brothers and with the flocks, and bring word back to me." Then he sent him out of the Valley of Hebron.

The Meaning of Shechem and What Jacob Knew

Why are we informed that the tribes were herding the sheep in Shechem? Why Shechem? Could they not have gone elsewhere, since Shechem was quite far away? Why did Jacob send Joseph to join his brothers—did he not know that his other sons hated Joseph?

Joseph answered with, "I am here" not "I am ready," thereby indicating his level of consciousness. The city of Shechem encompasses the energy of Yesod, and Joseph knew he had to connect to this place. When we listen to this reading on Shabbat, we have the opportunity to connect with the city of Shechem and the Sefira of Yesod, and also be unified in spirit with Joseph the Righteous. This whole story is a code for understanding the nature of reality.

When Joseph arrived at Shechem, 15 a man found him wandering around in the fields and asked him, "What are you looking for?" 16 He replied, "I'm looking for my brothers. Can you tell me where they are feeding their flocks?" 17 "They have moved on from here," the man answered. "I heard them say, 'Let's go to Dothan.' " So Joseph went after his brothers and found them near Dothan. 18 But they saw him in the distance, and before he reached them, they plotted to kill him. 19 "Here comes that dreamer!" they said to each other. 20 "Come now, let's kill him and throw him into one of these cisterns and say that a ferocious animal devoured him. Then we'll see what comes of his dreams." 21 When Reuben heard this, he tried to rescue him from their hands. "Let's not take his life," he said. 22 "Don't shed any blood. Throw him into this cistern here in the desert, but don't lay a hand on him." Reuben said this to rescue him from them and take him back to his father. 23 So when Joseph came to his brothers, they stripped him of his robe, the striped robe he was wearing, 24 and they took him and threw him into the cistern. Now the cistern was empty; there was no water in it. 25 As they sat down to eat their meal, they looked up and saw a caravan of Ishmaelites coming from Gilead. Their camels were loaded with spices, balm, and myrrh, and they were on their way to take them down to Egypt. 26 Judah said to his brothers, "What will we gain if we kill our brother and cover

up his blood? 27 Come, let's sell him to the Ishmaelites and not lay our hands on him; after all, he is our brother, our own flesh and blood." His brothers agreed. 28 So when the Midianite merchants came by, his brothers pulled Joseph up out of the cistern and sold him for twenty shekels of silver to the Ishmaelites, who took him to Egypt.

Joseph's Fate to go into Egypt

How could the Shechinah be involved in this kidnapping? The Zohar explains that if Joseph's brothers did not sell him and get him to Egypt, and if Joseph had not reached the level of closeness to Pharaoh, then when the time came, the Israelites could not have escaped from Egypt. If Joseph had gone to Egypt by his own doing, without having been sold into slavery and without going through the trials that he experienced, the energy would have been foreign and he would never have been able to get out. This is a lesson for all of us. Sometimes what may seem like the end of a road is in fact just the beginning.

It is incomprehensible that Joseph's brothers, who are Chariots—conduits of the Light—would sell him. Why is there so much apparent hatred in this portion? There is also hatred found in the story about Jacob and Leah. Why is Leah despised? She had seven children with Jacob—six boys and one girl. There is an explanation for this in the Zohar. When hatred is mentioned in the Bible, it is referring to an imbalance of form, meaning different levels of consciousness. In the case of Joseph and his brothers, the brothers were masters of Malchut, the dimension of Kingdom—the physical world; whereas Joseph was connected to Zeir Anpin. As we discussed previously, Joseph's striped coat denotes "voice," which is a code for Zeir Anpin—Small Face. Jacob knew that Joseph had the capacity to transfer the energy of the Lightforce of God from Zeir Anpin to Malchut (from Small Face to Kingdom), and this is why he gave him the striped coat. The jealousy and hatred was not about the coat but about the various ways in which functions exist in the system.

The Bible deals with matters of consciousness, not with material substance. Quantum science essentially agrees that physicality is just an interference in the fabric of consciousness. When we see a human being, it is really only an indication that consciousness is present there. For example, when we visit the grave of a righteous person, we are not connecting with what remains there physically but rather we connect with his spiritual essence. Some of the righteous are buried on a mountain or in a ravine—places that are hard to reach. Such remote locations are used so that we come to understand that there is consciousness in these places, an energy that one must first discover to connect with it. Similarly, the instant the physical body has a problem, such as an illness, consciousness has to take over and declare to the malady, "Go away, get out of here."

By law, selling someone into slavery warrants the punishment of a death sentence; so we cannot take it literally that these chariots would do such a thing. It is a ridiculous story, and one of the most challenging chapters to understand in the entire Bible.

The Zohar explains that the Israelites (all the children of the twelve tribes) were destined to go down into Egypt and become slaves. This was the covenant that Abraham made with God, and from which ultimately emerged the holiday of Passover (Heb. Pesach). The Zohar says that this traumatic event had to happen. Without Rav Ashlag's (1885 – 1954) commentary on the Zohar, I would be unable to give an explanation for this portion. The Zohar says that here we see destiny at work: Joseph had to be sold into slavery to the Egyptians to enable the unfolding of momentous events that would follow. Joseph was not sold by chance; it was predestined that he be brought into Egypt, and that there would be a great famine all around the world. It was foretold that the only food for the entire world would be found in Egypt. Joseph had to go there so that the Israelites themselves would ultimately also have to go into the land of Egypt.

If the brothers did not have power over Joseph then Egypt would not have power over Israel—and there would be no redemption. We do know that as soon as Joseph died, hard times began for the Israelites.

Sale of a Brother

This section is so inconceivable that if understood only superficially, it would be read with disgust. The Holy Bible—not the Holy Grail, which is the Zohar—says that ten of Jacob's sons elected to sell their brother into slavery. There was a point when they thought of killing Joseph because their father showed him preference.

We are not discussing regular human beings here. We are talking about people who are physical, rational beings, but are also able to adjust the physical realm and thereby co-exist with the immaterial dimension—the real world we know as the 99 Percent Reality. Such a person is a Chariot, a Patriarch, like Abraham, Isaac and, of course, Jacob.

True understanding of this story's meaning comes only from the Zohar. The Zohar tells us that Jacob is in control of chaos. He represents the Central Column of the Upper Worlds. The Central Column of the lower aspect of the triad is Joseph. This is the power of the technology of the Magen David (Shield of David). The Bible is so abstruse, says the Zohar, that we cannot understand one word if we only read it superficially.

Although initially I could never understand the sale of one brother by another, the Zohar explained it to me. The ultimate and only objective of the Zohar and the Bible is to teach us the spiritual rules, laws, and principles—the mechanics of the universe that show us how we can remove chaos.

When I came to California in 1983, someone told me a story about how his father became blind. His father and his uncle were partners in the ownership of a building. In the midst of a heated disagreement, his uncle became so incensed that he threw acid in his father's eyes. I could not imagine that one brother could do such a thing to another. Satan will go to any lengths to sow chaos and discord in our lives. The story of Joseph and his brothers wants to teach us that in the physical world, where we hold our rational minds in high esteem, a brother can indeed sell another brother. In the world of chaos, there is no love.

When we live in a non-spiritual atmosphere and consciousness, anything can happen—even to the extent that we could wish to harm those who are very close to us. We must never be in denial that Satan can play any number of tricks on us in this Malchut reality. The Bible is teaching us that we have to make every effort to become like these Chariots, so we can rise above this level of Malchut. Each son of Jacob participated in the grand scheme of the cosmos. The twelve signs of the zodiac greatly affect us. Each month provides us with very specific aspects of the Light, and astrology creates and forms our personal characteristics. Without the integration of the spiritual dimension, nothing is true; nothing is meaningful unless spirit is integrated into it. The reason the spiritual is so called is because the spirit does not have limitations.

The 99 Percent Reality is not confined to the restrictions of time, space, and motion.

29 When Reuben returned to the cistern and saw that Joseph was not there, he tore his clothes. 30 He went back to his brothers and said, "The boy isn't there! Where can I turn now?" 31 Then they got Joseph's robe, slaughtered a goat, and dipped the robe in the blood. 32 They took the striped robe back to their father and said, "We found this. Examine it to see whether it is your son's robe." 33 He recognized it and said, "It is my son's robe! Some ferocious animal has devoured him. Joseph has surely been torn to pieces." 34 Then Jacob tore his clothes, put on sackcloth, and mourned for his son many days. 35 All his sons and daughters came to comfort him, but he refused to be comforted. "No," he said, "in mourning will I go down to the grave to my son." So his father wept for him. 36 Meanwhile, the Midianites sold Joseph in Egypt to Potiphar, one of Pharaoh's officials, the captain of the guard.

Jacob's Deception, Tikkun, and Understanding

Just as Jacob deceived his father with Esau's clothing, so he in turn was deceived by his own children with Joseph's clothes. It is clear that this story is here to teach us about cause and effect, and *tikkun* (spiritual correction).

When the brothers asked Jacob, "...is this your son's robe?" Jacob answered, "...a wild animal had devoured Joseph." This answer indicates that Jacob understood this was as a result of the clothes he had worn when he deceived his own father.

For 3,400 years we have come to believe that Jacob the Patriarch, the Chariot of Tiferet, could not see whether his son, Joseph, was alive, and that he succumbed to depression, a state of consciousness to be expected of any father who has lost a son. Why could he no longer see the whole picture? Why could he not see the truth?

What is being discussed here is how we mortals will rid ourselves of the limitations of time, space, and motion. The power of the Torah Scroll becomes a part of us so that when we hear the reading of it, it will not leave us. Jacob had to wait seventeen years before he became aware that Joseph was alive. Jacob exists in two realms: There is Israel (elevated consciousness), and there is Jacob. The Bible uses the name Jacob here, despite the fact that his name was no longer Jacob, to show us his lower level of consciousness at this particular time. The Bible continues to refer to him as Jacob although he had shed that name because, while he had lost the name Israel, he did not lose it at the same time because he was a Chariot and could combine both worlds.

Beresheet 38:1 At that time, Judah left his brothers and went down to stay with a man of Adullam named Hirah. 2 There Judah met the daughter of a Canaanite man named Shua. He married her and lay with her; 3 she became pregnant and gave birth to a son, who was named Er. 4 She conceived again and gave birth to a son and named him Onan. 5 She gave birth to yet another son and named him Shelah. It was at Kezib that she gave birth to him. 6 Judah got a wife for Er, his firstborn, and her name was Tamar. 7 But Er, Judah's firstborn, was wicked in the Lord's sight; so the Lord put him to death. 8 Then Judah said to Onan, "Lie with your brother's wife and fulfill your duty to her as a brother-in-law to produce offspring for your brother." 9 But Onan knew that the offspring would not be his; so whenever he lay with his brother's wife, he spilled his semen on the ground to keep from producing offspring for his brother. 10 What he did was wicked in the Lord's sight; so He put him to death also. 11 Judah then said to his daughter-in-law Tamar, "Live as a widow in your father's house until my son Shelah grows up." For he thought, "He may die too, just like his brothers." So Tamar went to live in her father's house. 12 After a long time, Judah's wife, the daughter of Shua, died. When Judah had recovered from his grief, he went up to Timnah, to the men who were shearing his sheep, and his friend Hirah the Adullamite went with him. 13 When Tamar was told, "Your father-in-law is on his way to Timnah to shear his sheep," 14 she took off her widow's clothes, covered herself with a veil to disguise herself, and then sat down at the entrance to Enaim, which is on the road to Timnah. For she saw that though Shelah had now grown up she had not been given to him as his wife. 15 When Judah saw her, he thought she was a prostitute, for she had covered her face. 16 Not realizing that she was his daughter-in-law, he went over to her by the roadside and said, "Come now, let me sleep with you." "And what will you give me to sleep with you?" she asked. 17 "I'll send you a young goat from my flock," he said. "Will you give me something as a pledge until you send it?" she asked. 18 He said, "What pledge should I give you?" "Your seal and its cord, and the staff in your hand," she answered. So he gave them to her and slept with her, and she became pregnant by him. 19 After she left, she took off her veil and put on her widow's clothes again. 20 Meanwhile Judah sent the young goat by his friend the Adullamite in order to get his pledge back from the woman, but he did not find her. 21 He asked the men who lived there, "Where is the shrine prostitute who was beside the road at Enaim?" "There hasn't been any shrine prostitute here," they said. 22 So he went back to Judah and said, "I didn't find her. Besides, the men who lived there said, 'There hasn't been any shrine prostitute here.' " 23 Then Judah said, "Let her keep what she has, or we will become a laughingstock. After all, I did send her this young goat, but you didn't find her." 24 About three months later Judah was told, "Your daughter-in-law Tamar is guilty of prostitution, and as a result she is now pregnant." Judah said, "Bring her out and have her burned to death!" 25 As she was being brought out, she sent a message to her father-in-law. "I am pregnant by the man who owns these," she said. And she added, "See if you recognize whose seal and cord and staff these are." 26 Judah recognized them and said, "She is more righteous than I, since I wouldn't give her to my son Shelah." And he did not sleep with her again. 27 When the time came for her to give birth, there were twin boys in her womb. 28 As she was giving birth, one of them put out his hand; so the midwife took a scarlet thread and tied it on his wrist and said, "This one came out first." 29 But when he drew back his hand, his brother came out, and she said, "How you have broken out?" And he was named Perez. 30 Then his brother, who had the scarlet thread on his wrist, came out and he was given the name Zerah.

Judah, Tamar and the Soulmate Marriage

There are two surprisingly ribald stories in this chapter, the first with Judah and Tamar, and the second with Joseph and Potiphar's beautiful wife. The Bible seems here to be like every modern movie that has an obligatory sex scene.

This section concerns Judah, who married a woman and had three sons. Judah took a wife—Tamar—but his eldest son but this son died childless. Judah then had his second son marry Tamar; but this son, too, died childless. Judah was apprehensive about giving his third son to Tamar because she may have had the so-called "kiss of death." According to the Bible, a woman who is widowed twice is deemed fatal and is to be wary of.

Judah told Tamar to go back to her parents and that when his third son grew up, she could then become his wife. After some time, Judah's wife died. Judah traveled to the city of Timnah, where Tamar, his daughter-in-law, heard of his arrival, and she took off her widow's clothes, putting a veil over herself so that he would not recognize her, and then posed as a prostitute at the gates of the city. Tamar made sure he mistook her for a prostitute. Judah did what many lonely men do; when he saw a prostitute he wanted to utilize her services. She took his seal from him, and other items to ensure payment. And later, when they wanted to burn her for prostitution, Tamar showed him the seal and those other items, and said these all belonged to the man with whom she had had relations. Judah recognized his belongings, and there was no question, says the Zohar, that Judah understood he had been punished because he did not give Tamar his youngest son in marriage. Following this encounter, they had no further relations but Tamar conceived twins from the one initial encounter.

This story is filled with confusion, hypocrisy, and distortion—things we are all guilty of now and then. The Bible is unafraid of presenting life in the raw. However, the Zohar says there is a deeper significance to this story. What is being discussed here is the origin of soulmates.

The Zohar gives us an unusual interpretation of the story. From the sexual relationship between Judah and Tamar was born the origin of what would ultimately be the *Mashiach* (Messiah). Tamar gave birth to twins, one of whom would become the great-grandfather of King David. The holy Zohar says that between Tamar and Judah there was a soulmate connection. Looking at the context of their relationship, it is hard to believe that this could be so. What are we to think of a patriarch going to bed with a prostitute because he was depressed, and then wanting to burn his daughter-in-law? The Zohar brings the idea that, in this physical universe, there exists something known as soulmates. The Zohar says the Bible cannot be read only literally, just as stories—although it is possible to learn from scripture to a degree even on the basic story level.

This portion is giving us the technology whereby soulmates can be found. Rav Isaac Luria (the Ari, 1534 – 1572) said soulmates only come from irrational encounters, such as Tamar and Judah's meeting at the city gates. The Ari explains even further that, if the husband and wife come from the same place, grow up together and go to the same school, they are probably not soulmates. The reading of this section enables people to obtain the energy to better see a real mate, which is very difficult in this modern society of ours, where everything is measured by material standards.

Tamar was Judah's destined mate; but it was not the most auspicious beginning in which the House of David was established. When we talk about true love, it is not what we have become familiar with these days, such as love between colleagues, or between two people who have fun together, or who help each other. True partners build a life together, although it may not be easy, and the love might not always be evident.

Tamar was truly righteous, and she realized that Judah was her soulmate and that the House of David and the *Mashiach* would come from her descendants. This is why she did what she did. Here we see the difference between a man and a woman. Tamar saw clearly that Judah was her mate. While, on the contrary, he not only did not see it, he also wanted to have her burned.

This story informs us why women are more attracted to spirituality than men, and why women do not have to return in different bodies to perfect themselves. The only reason women return in a new incarnation is for the *tikkun* (spiritual correction) of their mate. For this reason, I recommend to women that they do not complain about the man they have, since they did not have to come back here for their own benefit—but for his. This portion helps us to receive the power to be connected to our true mate, and also to be connected to the right partners in business and other relationships.

Beresheet 39:1 Now Joseph had been taken down to Egypt. Potiphar, an Egyptian who was one of Pharaoh's officials, the captain of the guard, bought him from the Ishmaelites who had taken him there. 2 The Lord was with Joseph and he prospered, and he lived in the house of his Egyptian master. 3 When his master saw that the Lord was with him and that the Lord gave him success in everything he did, 4 Joseph found favor in his eyes and became his attendant. Potiphar put him in charge of his household, and he entrusted to his care everything he owned. 5 From the time he put him in charge of his household and of all that he owned, the Lord blessed the household of the Egyptian because of Joseph. The blessing of the Lord was on everything Potiphar had, both in the house and in the field. 6 So he left in Joseph's care everything he had; with Joseph in charge, he did not concern himself with anything except the food he ate. Now Joseph was well-built and handsome, 7 and after a while his master's wife took notice of Joseph and said, "Come to bed with me!" 8 But he refused. "With me in charge," he told her, "my master does not concern himself with anything in the house; everything he owns he has entrusted to my care. 9 No one is greater in this house than I am. My master has withheld nothing from me except you, because you are his wife. How then could I do such a wicked thing and sin against God?" 10 And though she spoke to Joseph day after day, he refused to go to bed with her or even be with her. 11 One day he went into the house to attend to his duties, and none of the household servants was inside. 12 She caught him by his cloak and said, "Come to bed with me!" But he left his cloak in her hand and ran out of the house. 13 When she saw that he had left his cloak in her hand and had run out of the house, 14 she called her household servants. "Look," she said to them, "this Hebrew has been brought to us to make fun of us! He came in here to sleep with me, but I screamed out. 15 When he heard me scream for help, he left his cloak beside me and ran out of the house." 16 She kept his cloak beside her until his master came home. 17 Then she told him this story: "That Hebrew slave you brought us came to me to mock me. 18 But as soon as I screamed for help, he left his cloak beside me and ran out of the house." 19 When his master heard the story his wife told him, saying, "This is how your slave treated me," he burned with anger. 20 Joseph's master took him and put him in prison, the place where the king's prisoners were confined. But while Joseph was there in the prison, 21 the Lord was with him; He showed him kindness and granted him favor in the eyes of the prison warden. 22 So the warden put Joseph in charge of all those held in the prison, and he was made responsible for all that was done there. 23 The warden paid no attention to anything under Joseph's care, because the Lord was with

Joseph and gave him success in whatever he did.

Joseph Became a Tzadik by Restricting

The Bible is far from dull. Here it tells us about a beautiful woman who wanted to seduce Joseph. However, Joseph restricted his desire for her, and he resisted her advances, thereby becoming Joseph the Righteous (Heb. *Yosef Ha Tzadik*). From this restriction, Joseph emerged as the foundation and source of the Sefira of Yesod. We make every effort, in all of our connections with the Light, to unite Yesod with the material world—the world of chaos—so the Light of Yesod will have dominion and will banish chaos forever.

In this chapter, it is clear how Joseph elevated from Joseph to Joseph the Righteous. He was presented with the opportunity to cleanse when he was given the test with Potiphar's wife. What tremendous resistance that must have required!

Joseph understood that the only real power in this world is the Light—everything else is only a vessel for the Light. In fact, in looking closely at the unfolding of events, it was this one that established Joseph as a ruler. The story of Joseph teaches us that a person sometimes has to sink very low to rise. Joseph's strength was in his knowing that whatever happened was ultimately beneficial to him and that everyone he met served as a channel for him.

When we are confronted with difficulties, problems, pain or suffering, it is the power of resistance that is necessary to overcome such chaos. Joseph had to be sold into slavery. Was he truly a slave when he was in charge of Potiphar's house? Did he really have trouble with Potiphar's wife? Joseph was above all of it. He was sold as a slave and became a viceroy. The Bible presents us with all of this so that we can tap into the energy of the Central Column; so we can reflect on the coming week, the coming year or the next five years with consciousness and the power of Joseph. Vayeshev provides incredible wisdom that should not be lost or wasted on us.

Joseph was imprisoned and immediately thereafter, became the master of his prison. If we are like Joseph, we, too, can have chaos all around us and still be in control. Joseph refused temptation and put up restriction. Because of this act of restriction he became Joseph the Righteous. We all have the potential to become a *tzadik* (righteous person) but it comes about only with a connection to the Flawless Universe, the only place where there is perfection.

Did you ever notice that when it comes to our own personal chaos, we all compete to say ours is the worst possible chaos?

Restriction is how Joseph connected and elevated to the realm of Yesod—outside the dimension of the physical reality. He was no longer himself, he was now a *tzadik*. Knowing about Restriction, about the aspect of the Central Column, is what brings the highest dimensionality to the immune system, enabling us to remove our chaos, which in effect means we are outside of that chaos. We are right now in the era of the Woe and Praiseworthy. We are in the era of the Final Redemption. We can create a shield around ourselves and become non-judgmental, resisting the temptations we face. In other words, we can now restrict. The energy to restrict is what it is possible for us to absorb with this reading.

The story of Joseph teaches us that our misery and chaos, and how we deal with them, are all in our hands. Our frame of mind can transmute our experience from one of suffering to one of wisdom received from the Upper Realm. When we see that our suffering has been of our own making and then transform it by taking responsibility to infuse that suffering with Light, we can raise ourselves to the level of a *tzadik* and be a channel to reach that level where suffering can be transformed into happiness. This reading enables our connection to the quantum world. Theoretically, quantum is correct but science has yet to accept the concept.

What does quantum mean? It means that if you put a drop of water into a lake, it affects the whole lake. Science proclaims that the droplet should dilute itself in the greater waters. But when scientists put a drop of dye into a body of water to see where the original drop would travel, they found that it does not, in fact, travel at all. The dye becomes part of the place in which it is dropped, and does not move around. Another problem with quantum is that it eliminates time, space, and motion. For example, a drop of water can travel all around the world faster than the speed of light. And anything that can travel faster than the speed of light can go back in time. So then destiny itself becomes a problem.

Why should a murderer go free if there were a thousand witnesses to his crime? Because he had no choice—it was destined for him to kill? This is a flaw in the quantum theory because quantum eliminates time, space, and motion. This is what the Zohar tells us: It was the destiny of the Israelites to be slaves. Hence, the children of Jacob were merely playing out a part, like the man on trial for murder, who claims that he was merely playing out the part of a murderer.

If one tries to live with this opinion, it perpetuates the notion that there is no pure, beneficial, sharing aspect of God in this universe. We could say to ourselves that we cannot escape from the chaos that exists—for it is our destiny. Yet what the Zohar is saying is that we can walk out of one universe into another. The Zohar reveals that there are indeed parallel universes.

The Reward for Suffering

The Zohar raises a very important question about the destruction of the Temple and Rabbi Akiva (Akiva ben Yosef, 50 – 137 AD). The Romans killed Rabbi Akiva by flaying him alive with an iron comb that scraped and tore the flesh. We know how painful a blister can be when the skin is torn off. But this is what the Romans did to Rabbi Akiva—they removed the skin from his entire body. How could God have let this happen to a man like Rabbi Akiva? How could there be any justification for such negativity inflicted upon a man whom Rav Shimon says was the greatest soul that ever lived? In fact Rav Shimon asked God: "Why me, why should I be the one to reveal the Zohar when you have Rabbi Akiva to reveal it?" Such was the spiritual level of Rabbi Akiva, so why was such a death his reward? Rav Shimon provides an answer that has infinite layers to it. He said that Rabbi Akiva knew he was one of the ten brothers of Joseph, and that he came back to atone for the act of selling Joseph. The moment the Romans began to scrape off his skin, Rabbi Akiva asked them to give him more pain because he knew it was for the purpose of cleansing.

There is a story that illustrates what is taking place spiritually when we experience a cleansing. In old Russia, there was a man who received one hundred lashings while his master was away on business. Upon returning, this master, the lord of the manor, saw his servant crying and asked what had happened. The man replied that he was lashed one hundred times by those who were left in charge. So the lord gave the man one hundred rubles in total, one ruble for each lashing. Then the man arrived at his own home still sobbing. His wife asked him if he had been lashed again. "No," he answered, "The lord rewarded me with one hundred rubles, one for each lashing. I am crying because I wish they had beaten me more."

We need to elevate ourselves to the point where it can be understood that suffering is part of a cleansing, that negativity is not something that comes randomly, and that, when it comes, it has to be dealt with. Rabbi Akiva dealt with it by connecting to that other universe, where the purpose of such things is understood. The moment he said, "Give me more pain" his soul left his body, as the Romans still continued to peel off his skin. Rav Shimon had the same thought about the fire that destroyed the Holy Temple; when something is preordained, it is because a cleansing is required from actions in this or another lifetime. Nothing is random; everything is quantum—and quantum is not random. This is the level of consciousness Rabbi Akiva attained.

Rather than whining, we should look at what is happening to us. Nothing happens without a reason, and it is only those who are destined to suffer with their iniquities who blame others. Rabbi Akiva showed us how to experience our whole lives with his painful execution. It is the way we should treat our own brothers and families too. But we all continue to think we are so pure; we believe we are right, and that the other person is always wrong. Some people will even give up a business because they are right and want support for their position of imagined "rectitude."

When Jacob gave that famous coat to Joseph, he invested in hatred for no reason even when he knew that the result would be suffering. In this physical world, Satan is the ruler. But make no mistake about it, there is another universe—a parallel, immaterial one known as the Flawless Universe—where we can leave this darkened realm with all of its hate and chaos. This portion gives us the strength to deal with our chaos and take responsibility, with no more excuses, whining or complaining.

Beresheet 40:1 Sometime later, the cupbearer and the baker of the king of Egypt offend-
ed their master, the king of Egypt. 2 Pharaoh
was angry with his two officials, the chief
cupbearer and the chief baker, 3 and put
them in custody in the house of the captain of
the guard, in the same prison where Joseph
was confined. 4 The captain of the guard as-
signed them to Joseph, and he attended them.
After they had been in custody for some time,
5 each of the two men—the cupbearer and
the baker of the king of Egypt, who were being held in prison—had a dream the same
night, and each dream had a meaning of its
own. 6 When Joseph came to them the next
morning, he saw that they were dejected. 7 So
he asked Pharaoh's officials who were in custody with him in his master's house, "Why
are your faces so sad today?" 8 "We both had
dreams," they answered, "but there is no one
to interpret them." Then Joseph said to them,
"Do not interpretations belong to God? Tell
me your dreams." 9 So the chief cupbearer
told Joseph his dream. He said to him, "In
my dream I saw a vine in front of me, 10 and
on the vine were three branches. As soon as
it budded, it blossomed, and its clusters rip-
ened into grapes. 11 Pharaoh's cup was in my
hand, and I took the grapes, squeezed them
into Pharaoh's cup and put the cup in his
hand." 12 "This is what it means," Joseph
said to him. "The three branches are three
days. 13 Within three days Pharaoh will lift
up your head and restore you to your posi-

tion and you will put Pharaoh's cup in his hand, just as you used to do when you were his cupbearer. 14 But when all goes well with you, remember me and show me kindness; mention me to Pharaoh and get me out of this prison. 15 For I was forcibly carried off from the land of the Hebrews, and even here I have done nothing to deserve being put in a dungeon." 16 When the chief baker saw that Joseph had given a favorable interpretation, he said to Joseph, "I too had a dream: On my head were three baskets of bread. 17 In the top basket were all kinds of baked goods for Pharaoh, but the birds were eating them out of the basket on my head." 18 "This is what it means," Joseph said. "The three baskets are three days. 19 Within three days Pharaoh will lift off your head and hang you on a tree. And the birds will eat away your flesh." 20 Now the third day was Pharaoh's birthday, and he gave a feast for all his officials. He lifted up the heads of the chief cupbearer and the chief baker in the presence of his officials: 21 He restored the chief cupbearer to his position, so that he once again put the cup into Pharaoh's hand, 22 but he hanged the chief baker, just as Joseph had said to them in his interpretation. 23 The chief cupbearer, however, did not remember Joseph; he forgot him.

The Dreamers and the Redemption

It must be remembered that the people who were in jail with Joseph, the people who had the dreams, were very close to Pharaoh. This was the cause of the redemption of all the people of Israel. The Zohar explains that a dream is like prophecy, and that the soul, however, must leave the body to connect with that kind of information. The Zohar further explains that sometimes the information we receive in a dream is entirely correct and that sometimes only a part of it is true, and the other part is illusion.

Joseph had the opportunity to interpret the dreams of the baker and cupbearer (or wine steward). He asked this chief wine steward to remember him to Pharaoh when the man saw his dream come true. Yet the wine steward did not do as he had promised he would. This is a little reminder for us that no person can lift us out of chaos—not our lawyers, accountants or our rabbis. The only one who can lift us out of chaos is ourselves—and we do it by connecting to the Light. The wine steward depended on Joseph's interpretation but he forgot Joseph once he was released from prison, and Joseph remained there for another two years. What can be gleaned from this is that salvation comes only from the Lightforce of God—no one or nowhere else can effect it.

Conclusion

There are 112 verses in this chapter, which is the numerological value (Heb. *gematria*) of Elohim (86) and the Tetragrammaton (26); and it is also the connection between the material world, the world of judgment, and the spiritual world, the world of compassion and mercy. It is not by chance that the sages specifically chose to have 112 verses in the portion of Vayeshev, which is all about compassion having power over judgment—the power of the brothers over Joseph—so that Egypt would not have power later on.

Joseph was away from Jacob for seventeen years, just as Jacob was away from *his* father, Isaac, for seventeen years. The whole narrative of what Jacob did to his father mirrors what happened with Joseph. As it will be recalled, Jacob was away from Isaac's home for twenty-two years; however, for five of those years, he was studying spiritual matters, so they do not count, making the number also seventeen.

The lesson for us here is that what we do today may make its mark or reveal its consequences only in many years to come. With any short circuit that we create, we are responsible for it—even if its consequences only arrive later on. Anything positive we do may also have its fruit in the future; and because of this, we have to pay close attention at all times to what we are doing. This is the quintessential message of Vayeshev.

About the Centres

Kabbalah is the deepest and most hidden meaning of the Torah or Bible. Through the ultimate knowledge and mystical practices of Kabbalah, one can reach the highest spiritual levels attainable. Although many people rely on belief, faith, and dogmas in pursuing the meaning of life, Kabbalists seek a spiritual connection with the Creator and the forces of the Creator, so that the strange becomes familiar, and faith becomes knowledge.

Throughout history, those who knew and practiced the Kabbalah were extremely careful in their dissemination of the knowledge because they knew the masses of mankind had not yet prepared for the ultimate truth of existence. Today, kabbalists know that it is not only proper but necessary to make the Kabbalah available to all who seek it.

The Research Centre of Kabbalah is an independent, non-profit institute founded in Israel in 1922. The Centre provides research, information, and assistance to those who seek the insights of Kabbalah. The Centre offers public lectures, classes, seminars, and excursions to mystical sites at branches in Israel and in the United States. Branches have been opened in Mexico, Montreal, Toronto, Paris, Hong Kong, and Taiwan.

Our courses and materials deal with the Zoharic understanding of each weekly portion of the Torah. Every facet of life is covered and other dimensions, hithertofore unknown, provide a deeper connection to a superior reality. Three important beginner courses cover such aspects as: Time, Space and Motion; Reincarnation, Marriage, Divorce; Kabbalistic Meditation; Limitation of the Five Senses; Illusion-Reality; Four Phases; Male and Female, Death, Sleep, Dreams; Food; and Shabbat.

Thousands of people have benefited from the Centre's activities, and the Centre's publishing of kabbalistic material continues to be the most comprehensive of its kind in the world, including translations in English, Hebrew, Russian, German, Portuguese, French, Spanish, Farsi (Persian).

Kabbalah can provide one with the true meaning of their being and the knowledge necessary for their ultimate benefit. It can show one spirituality that is beyond belief. The Research Centre of Kabbalah will continue to make available the Kabbalah to all those who seek it.

—Rav Berg, 1984

About The Zohar

The Zohar, the basic source of the Kabbalah, was authored two thousand years ago by Rabbi Shimon bar Yochai while hiding from the Romans in a cave in Peki'in for 13 years. It was later brought to light by Rabbi Moses de Leon in Spain, and further revealed through the Safed Kabbalists and the Lurianic system of Kabbalah.

The programs of the Research Centre of Kabbalah have been established to provide opportunities for learning, teaching, research, and demonstration of specialized knowledge drawn from the ageless wisdom of the Zohar and the Jewish sages. Long kept from the masses, today this knowledge of the Zohar and Kabbalah should be shared by all who seek to understand the deeper meaning of this spiritual heritage, and a deeper and more profound meaning of life. Modern science is only beginning to discover what our sages veiled in symbolism. This knowledge is of a very practical nature and can be applied daily for the betterment of our lives and of humankind.

Darkness cannot prevail in the presence of Light. Even a darkened room must respond to the lighting of a candle. As we share this moment together we are beginning to witness, and indeed some of us are already participating in, a people's revolution of enlightenment. The darkened clouds of strife and conflict will make their presence felt only as long as the Eternal Light remains concealed.

The Zohar now remains an ultimate, if not the only, solution to infusing the cosmos with the revealed Lightforce of the Creator. The Zohar is not a book about religion. Rather, the Zohar is concerned with the relationship between the unseen forces of the cosmos, the Lightforce, and the impact on humanity.

The Zohar promises that with the ushering in of the Age of Aquarius, the cosmos will become readily accessible to human understanding. It states that in the days of the Messiah "there will no longer be the necessity for one to request of his neighbor, teach me wisdom." (Zohar, Naso 9:65) "One day, they will no longer teach every man his neighbor and every man his brother, saying know the Lord. For they shall all know Me, from the youngest to the oldest of them." (Jeremiah 31:34)

We can, and must, regain dominion of our lives and environment. To achieve this objective, the Zohar provides us with an opportunity to transcend the crushing weight of universal negativity.

The daily perusing of the Zohar, without any attempt at translation or understanding will fill our consciousness with the Light, improving our well-being, and influencing all in our environment toward positive attitudes. Even the scanning of the Zohar by those unfamiliar with the Hebrew *Alef Bet* will accomplish the same result.

The connection that we establish through scanning the Zohar is one of unity with the Light of the Creator. The letters, even if we do not consciously know Hebrew or Aramaic, are the channels through which the connection is made and can be likened to dialing the right telephone number or typing in the right codes to run a computer program. The connection is established at the metaphysical level of our being and radiates into our physical plane of existence. But first there is the prerequisite of metaphysical "fixing." We have to consciously, through positive thought and actions, permit the immense power of the Zohar to radiate love, harmony, and peace into our lives for us to share with all humanity and the universe.

As we enter the years ahead, the Zohar will continue to be a people's book, striking a sympathetic chord in the hearts and minds of those who long for peace, truth, and relief from suffering. In the face of crises and catastrophe, the Zohar has the ability to resolve agonizing human afflictions by restoring each individual's relationship with the Lightforce of the Creator.

—Rav Berg, 1984

Kabbalah Centre Books

72 Names of God, The: Technology for the Soul

72 Names of God for Kids, The: A Treasury of Timeless Wisdom

72 Names of God Meditation Book, The

And You Shall Choose Life: An Essay on Kabbalah, the Purpose of Life, and Our True Spiritual Work

Angel Intelligence: How Your Consciousness Determines Which Angels Come Into Your Life

AstrologiK: Kabbalistic Astrology Guide for Children

Becoming Like God: Kabbalah and Our Ultimate Destiny

Beloved of My Soul: Letters of Our Master and Teacher Rav Yehuda Tzvi Brandwein to His Beloved Student Kabbalist Rav Berg

Consciousness and the Cosmos (previously *Star Connection*)

Days of Connection: A Guide to Kabbalah's Holidays and New Moons

Days of Power Part 1

Days of Power Part 2

Dialing God: Daily Connection Book

Education of a Kabbalist

Energy of the Hebrew Letters, The (previously *Power of the Aleph Beth Vols. 1 and 2*)

Fear is Not an Option

Finding the Light Through the Darkness: Inspirational Lessons Rooted in the Bible and the Zohar

God Wears Lipstick: Kabbalah for Women

Holy Grail, The: A Manifesto on the Zohar

If You Don't Like Your Life, Change It!: Using Kabbalah to Rewrite the Movie of Your Life

Immortality: The Inevitability of Eternal Life

Kabbalah Connection, The: Preparing the Soul For Pesach

Kabbalah for the Layman

Kabbalah Method, The: The Bridge Between Science and the Soul, Physics and Fulfillment, Quantum and the Creator

Kabbalah on the Sabbath: Elevating Our Soul to the Light

Kabbalah: The Power To Change Everything

Kabbalistic Astrology: And the Meaning of Our Lives

Kabbalistic Bible: Genesis

Kabbalistic Bible: Exodus

Kabbalistic Bible: Leviticus

Kabbalistic Bible: Numbers

Kabbalistic Bible: Deuteronomy

Life Rules: How Kabbalah Can Turn Your Life From a Problem into a Solution

Living Kabbalah